Cyrus Sturdivant

Sketches of the Life and Work of Capt

Cyrus Sturdivant

Sketches of the Life and Work of Capt

ISBN/EAN: 9783743370982

Manufactured in Europe, USA, Canada, Australia, Japa

Cover: Foto ©Thomas Meinert / pixelio.de

Manufactured and distributed by brebook publishing software
(www.brebook.com)

Cyrus Sturdivant

Sketches of the Life and Work of Capt

SKETCHES OF THE LIFE AND WORK

OF

Capt. Cyrus Sturdivant

THE PRISONER'S FRIEND,

INCLUDING AN ACCOUNT OF THE RESCUE AND CONVERSION OF

FRANCIS MURPHY,

AND OTHERS;

*Also, Incidents of Capt. Sturdivant's Sea-going Life,
as well as his Illustrated Home Mission and
Gospel Temperance Work, Written by
Himself, with an Introduction by
Francis Murphy.*

———————

NEW YORK:
WILLIS McDONALD & Co., Printers,
19 Park Place.
———
1879,

PREFACE.

I have for a long time felt it my duty to give to the world an abridged history of my life, hoping it might influence the young to seek the religion of Christ, which would save them from a "thousand snares;" and especially desiring that the readers of the book might be prompted to use special efforts to redeem man from the terrible practice of using intoxicating drinks, and to help "rescue the perishing and lift up the fallen," I wish, therefore, to dedicate this little volume to the reformed men of this country, and to their families and friends who are now rejoicing in their new life of sobriety, and in the blessings resulting therefrom.

INTRODUCTION.

It is a great pleasure for me to write a few lines introducing this book to the reading public, containing as it does, a faithful account of the remarkable history on sea and land of a man who has traveled the ocean as sailor, and, by the faithful discharge of duty, won honorable distinction as captain of one of the finest steamers that ever sailed out of Portland harbor. Early converted to God, he gave Him his whole heart, and began to work for Him with wonderful success. When on shore, he could be found in the prayer-meeting presenting the Gospel of the world's Redeemer to the poor and needy. He had a mission chapel, which he supported for many years. There he gathered in God's needy ones.

Being a sailor, he knew how to cast his net on the right side of the Gospel ship, and always with great success. To the astonishment of many who had fished all night without success, the Captain had his net full.

Captain Sturdivant was anointed by God to preach good tidings to the meek. He came to bind up the broken-hearted, to proclaim liberty to the captives, and the opening of the prison house to them that were bound, dealing his bread to hungry, bringing the poor that were cast out to his house, clothing the naked—never hiding from his own flesh. He had a handsome fortune. He has given it all to God's poor. His treasure is laid up "where moth and rust doth not corrupt, and where thieves cannot break through and steal." Poor to-day in this world's goods, yet he is rich, possessing all things in the consciousness of duty done to his brother man. Thousands all over this land rise up to call him blessed.

I bespeak for his book a place in every home where the English language is read, confident it will bring a blessing to the heart and home. To this good Christian man am I indebted, under the blessing of God, for a knowledge of the saving power of the world's Redeemer in my heart. May God bless him, my dearest friend!

                                    FRANCIS MURPHY.

AUTOBIOGRAPHY

OF

Capt. CYRUS STURDIVANT.

CHAPTER I.

ON DECK.

I was born, and my boyhood days were spent, in the town of Cumberland, in the State of Maine, situated on the shore of Casco Bay, a beautiful sheet of water, containing 365 islands, just the number of days in a year.

At the age of fifteen years I trust I experienced religion during a "Protracted Meeting," at which meeting also a number of my young associates found the same blessed pearl of great price; and we together connected ourselves with the Methodist church, over which Rev. Joshua Taylor, one of the pioneer Methodist preachers in New England, was pastor. He has long since gone to his reward in heaven; and, it seems to me, if real goodness is rewarded hereafter, his reward will be very great. Many of my youthful associates have also passed over to the beautiful land; and those who, with myself, commenced thus early a religious life, have never regretted the decision we then made.

Soon after my conversion, my parents had a desire to give me a better education than could well be procured at our district school, and decided to send me to Kent's Hill Seminary, about sixty miles distant from my home, in company with several other boys from the neighborhood : in packing our little trunks for three months' absence, our parents not forgetting to put in with the clothing a Testament, and something good to eat, we left home in a stage-coach, as at that time the railroads in Maine were but few in number, and after a long and tedious ride, and to me a very lonesome journey, we arrived at Kent's Hill late in the evening, and I was landed at the door of my new home, to board in the family of Mr. Dudley Moody, who, with his estimable Christian wife, endeavored to make me feel contented and happy ; but did not succeed for several days, as I had a severe and continual attack of real *home-sickness ;* and those of my readers who have never suffered from the same cause cannot enter into sympathy with my first week's experience at Kent's Hill. Ere long, however, becoming acquainted with the boys and girls of the school, I felt more at home, and pursued my studies like a "good boy," as the teachers called me. Very foolishly I consented to stay only two terms at this excellent school, for I was so haunted with visions of " a life on the ocean wave," that at the close of my second term I returned to my home. My father, who was one of the most charitable men I ever knew, was in the United States Government service, as captain of a small cutter, a sailing vessel of about sixty tons measurement, and was employed in cruising in Casco bay and among the islands and harbors lying between Cape Elizabeth and Cape Small Point, on the coasts of Maine, to watch the cod fishermen, to see if they were entitled to the bounty money; as the United States Government at that time gave all fishing vessels employed fully four months in each year in cod fishing a bounty of eight dollars per ton measurement.

Serving as cabin-boy on board this small vessel for several years increased my desire for a sailor's life. While in this vessel I have known my father hundreds of times, in giving vent to his generous heart, visit harbors where lived very poor people, and from the stores (he finding them himself, not the Government), taking different kinds of provisions and giving them to these needy ones, and also giving away some of his own clothes and sometimes mine—which latter act I did not always concur in. I knew him on one occasion to take from his own feet a nice pair of boots, and give them to a poor man who had none. My father was an unselfish man, and I name these few facts to prove it; and also another fact and incident to show how earnestly he desired me to be unselfish, also, should God spare me to become a man. One day he took me to ride, I being only a lad of 12 years, through a neighborhood where lived a selfish man, as my father thought; and so, pointing out to me the residence, he says: "My son, a man who lives there has very narrow religious views, but he prays very regular every night and morning with his family and usually repeats the same prayer, viz: "Lord bless me and my wife, my son John and his wife, us four and no more. Amen."

After my father resigned his position as master of the cutter—for he was very conscientious about rotation in office—I went on board a packet schooner, plying between Portland and Boston, and continued for a few years, serving in the position of deck-hand and mate. My father, seeing my bent of mind, purchased for me a vessel suitable for the packeting and coasting business, and put me in command, procuring for me the services of an experienced man for mate.

During the few years intervening since my being at school at Kent's Hill, and taking command of the vessel spoken of, I was becoming more and more attached in my affections to a young lady, Amelia A. Poland, living in the neighborhood, and daughter of Captain Charles Poland, of Cumberland. To this excellant lady I was married when I was twenty-two years of age, and we lived very happily together for eight years; when after a long and distressing illness, she was called from this to the Land where death cannot enter. She died in the triumphs of faith; wondering why we, who were standing by her bed-side, could not hear the angels sing. We had four children given to us; two of which died in their infancy and purity, escaping the sins and ills and disappointments of this life; while the other two, a daughter and son, are still alive, the former residing in Maine and the latter in Colorado.

I continued in command of several sailing vessels and packets until I was invited by a new steamboat company to take charge of a propeller steamer; and I continued in command of this propeller, the "Commodore Preble," for seven years, plying between the cities of Portland and Boston. In about two years after the death of my wife, I was married again to Miss Ann S. Clarke, of Providence, R. I., whose acquaintance I formed while visiting some friends at Cambridgeport, Mass., and her worth and affection I prize more and more unto this day.

When the California gold fever first broke out, the "Commodore Preble" was sold to parties in New York to take passengers to that new country, and our steamboat company purchased a side-wheel steamer, the "John Marshall," and put me in command of her. In the summer season, on the coasts of Maine and Massachusetts, we have considerable foggy, although moderate, weather; but in the fall and winter and spring we often have severe gales and rough weather. I have been in trying and critical positions several times, when it would seem almost impossible to ride out the gale in safety. But He who holds the winds in His fists was our friend and deliverer, and we were brought out of trouble and danger, and are yet spared to work for Him. . . .

One instance of remarkable preservation I will name: One evening, early in the month of April, we left Portland, bound for Boston, in the side-wheel steamer St. Lawrence, under my command having on board about two hundred and thirty passengers, and a full cargo of freight. Nothing unusual occurred until we had been on our way about four hours, when suddenly the wind increased to a gale, and snow began to fall thick and fast; and after running on our course a few hours, daylight coming on, the gale still increasing, we could not discover the points of land we desired. The only safe and prudent alternative was for us to change the course of our steamer, and lay her off shore, head to the sea and storm, which was constantly increasing in roughness and fierceness. During the day one of our life-boats becoming partially loosened from her fastenings, one of the crew was ordered to secure it, and while doing so his foot slipped, and he fell overboard and was drowned; the sea being so rough and the storm so fierce that no earthly power could save him.

Just at dark, four or five hours before the fierceness of the storm abated, the Chief Engineer, Mr. George Cushing, came to report to me that he found the main steam pipe would give way and asked me what to do. I replied, you continue to do your duty as you always have done and we will all do the best we can, and so trust in God who holds the storms in his hands. He went to his engine room and from thence to the upper deck to cut away the canvass covering from what he feared was a weak point in the steam pipe—and then and there in the midst of the terrible storm and sea—bowed before God in prayer for our safety. He was and is now, one of the most devoted Christians I ever knew. During the following evening the storm abated, and the fog cleared away, and we found ourselves six miles north of the highland of Cape Cod, thankful to God that the gale had become a calm, and so we were saved from finding a watery grave, or being dashed upon the rough shore of the Cape, from whence there would have been no

escape. The next morning early we came safely
into Boston harbor, with the loss of large quanti-
ties of freight, which we threw overboard for the
safety of the steamer.

And now it was my painful duty to see at once
the wife and mother of the noble-hearted seaman
who perished while doing his duty in the midst of
the storm ; and to break to them the sad news of
his death ; which unexpected tidings fell heavy on
their crushed and loving hearts. He whom they
loved so well, and on whom they both depended
for earthly support, would be seen by them no more
until the sea gives up its dead.

During the storm there was terrible consternation
and alarm among some of the passengers. Prayers
could be heard coming from persons occupying the
state rooms, that God would spare them to meet
again loved ones at home, or to have mercy and
pardon and prepare them for Eternity, to which
they then felt they might soon be called.

In the ladies' cabin were two young ladies who
had left home contrary to the advice of their
widowed mother, to seek their fortune in the city of
Boston. These young ladies, feeling that perhaps
they might never see that mother again, cried unto
the Lord, and He heard their cries and forgave
their sins ; and they were both converted during
the storm, and took the first opportunity which

presented itself to return again to their Christian mother. How much better to give God our best affections in ' fair ~ weather, and to do nothing to grieve our mothers, whose love to us exceeds all other earthly love.

I continued as master of different steamers be-longing to the Portland Steam Packet Company for several years; but, finding the life was producing unhealthy symptoms in my constitution, I was ad-vised by my physician to procnre and engage in some other kind of business; and as soon as a good opportunity presented itself for business on shore, I availed myself of it. Being now in business in the city of Portland, I had opportuni-ties of attending church and Sabbath school, and other social means of grace, with regularity. I was soon called to official positions in the church and Sunday-school, in which positions I tried to be faithful. And now the home mission spirit (which had from the first, after my conversion, been a part of my make-up, not only in theory, but in practice, as my business and inter-course with my fellow-men presented opportunities,) seemed to have increasing facilities. While occupy-ing the position of Sabbath-school Superintendent in the church of my choice for several years, I felt there was urgent need of a mission school, as we had scores of earnest men and women who needed

such outside work for their own spiritual growth,
while hundreds of poor and neglected children were
living without the valuable blessing of Sabbath-
school instruction, and playing about the streets on
Sunday. But finding my own church at this time
not prepared to engage in such a work, I was called upon by the Young Men's Christian Association,
which had selected me for its President, to take
charge of a mission Sunday-school in the suburbs
of the city, which position as superintendent I occupied for two years, and the work was the delight
of my soul. Many of the children of the Deering's
Bridge Mission Sunday-school have grown to manhood and womanhood, and become useful in the
world, and bright and shining lights in the Church
of God on earth, while some of them have passed to
the better land. It is a great pleasure for me to
meet those who are now living, from time to time,
in the street or elsewhere. How delightful, also,
will it be for me to meet those over on the evergreen
shore, in the sweet by-and-by.

Soon after the expiration of my labors at the
Deering's Bridge Mission School my own church
took the work in hand of starting a mission Sunday-
school of their own. Having at this time a pastor
named Chas F. Allen, who favored the work, we
named the new organization the Allen Mission. The
first service was held in a small hall on Franklin

ALLEN MISSION CHAPEL.

street, which was furnished and fitted up by the Sunday-school of our church, and dedicated to the home mission work. After the expiration of only a few weeks from the dedication of our mission hall, the terrible fire of 1866 occurred at Portland, commencing July 4, which fire spread so fast and furious that all efforts of man proved unvailing to stop its terrible progress, until one-third of our beautiful Forest City was consumed, including the hall in which we held our mission services, and nearly all of the furniture and fixtures of the same. During the fire hundreds of poor families lost their dwellings and their all, and our mission work was of necessity greatly increased. The brethren and sisters, nothing daunted in their work of love, at once procured the loan of a canvass tent, which was soon erected and dedicated, and the poor children were collected in large numbers, the tent answering a good purpose until the weather became cold, and it was then thought best to hold the services in the chapel of the county jail, the use of which was cheerfully granted for two hours on each Sabbath afternoon.

After occupying the chapel of the jail for a few months, the school increased in numbers so rapidly that it was thought advisable to purchase or lease a lot of land, and to erect thereon a suitable chapel for our mission services and work. In a short time these plans were carried into effect, and a beautiful chapel was erected, which would seat comfortably about five hundred persons, and it was dedicated to the work and worship of Almighty God, and called the Allen Mission. God has made the Allen Mission the birth-place of many souls; and poor and hungry and ragged children, and also men and women have been here clothed and fed, and started on the way to sobriety and religion. My heart beats with gratitude to God when I look back and see all the way He has led us in our work at the Allen Mission. To Him be all the glory and honor.

Before proceeding to give an account of some of the interesting and wonderful conversions and incidents resulting, under God, from the faithful and continued labors of the Allen Mission workers, allow me to go back a little and state that, when I left the position as master of the Portland and Boston steamers, I engaged in business on Commercial street, Portland, as junior partner with Captain William Ross, one of God's noble men, and with whom I continued as associate for more than fifteen years in ship chandlery and commission and steamboat agency business. After an active life as master of vessels and a merchant of undoubted integrity, and a devoted Christian, two years ago he was called to his rest in heaven, leaving an interesting and afflicted family, a wife, two sons and two daughters to mourn his loss; and the writer feels-in the death of Captain Ross—the loss of one of his best friends —but he has gone where there is no more sea, to be with his Saviour and the loved children who passed on before.

The meetings at the Allen Mission Chapel, from its dedication, were marked with increasing numbers and increasing interest. The Sabbath-school which seemed for several years to be the most prominent part of the mission work, had a band of truly devoted and earnest Christian men and women as officers and teachers. I was honored first with the position of teacher, and then Assistant Superintendent. After about two years from the commencement of our work in the new chapel, the majority of the workers conceived the idea of forming a church out of the Mission. I was almost alone in opposing such a course, for I felt our own church ought to have a mission, and besides we had three Methodist churches which could accommodate a much larger number of persons than seemed desirous of attending at that time. The Maine Conference also deciding that it was not expedient to form another church out of the Mission, a large majority of the officers and teachers left the Sunday-school and the Mission work, to a *few* of us, and we toiled on trying to be faithful under this and many other discouragements; but the favor of God was so manifest, that we were not in the least discouraged. In a few months from this I was chosen Superintendent and Treasurer of the Allen Mission. We held at first only Sabbath-school services on Sunday at 3 P. M., and a social prayer meeting in the evening, and occasionally preaching from brethren in the ministry who might be in the city from time to time, and were willing and desirous to encourage us in our work; and some of these ministers seemed to esteem it a *privilege* to preach in the Allen Mission (as it really was); for on one occasion I asked a local elder to give us a sermon, and he complied with the request, and at the close of the services gave us ten dollars to help us in our work. The ladies of the Mission soon formed themselves into a regular organized society of workers, called the Allen Mission Sewing Circle; they met weekly, and sometimes oftener at their rooms in the chapel, to receive and disburse donations of cloth and clothing, and shoes and food, and other useful articles, which the good people sent in. The principal object of this Circle was to clothe the poor children, so they might be in a condition to come to Sunday-school and to worship. The kindness of those ladies did not stop with helping the children, but extended to the parents also, and to other adults who were needy; and in the Great Day to come hundreds will rise up and call those faithful and

untiring Christian women-workers, blessed. No
earthly compensation was received by any of the
laborers in the Allen Mission work. But the benediction of the Redeemer rested upon their hearts,
which to them was a satisfying portion. While writ-
ing these lines, I seem to see those faithful toilers
for the Master, in their working-room, fitting the
new garments to the dear little wanderers, who had
been clothed previously in rags. I see tears of joy
trickling down the cheeks of those Christian workers as the children danced with delight while being
provided with those new outfits. As I had opportunity, I would occasionally visit the near towns
and villages, giving the people some of my talks;
asking for contributions in money and clothing
to help us; and we never asked in vain. May
God abundantly bless the thousands of good
people who helped us at the Allen Mission, in
the great practical Gospel work of helping "feed
the hungry and clothe the naked!" Among the
many children who were thus helped was a little
girl, eleven years of age, who had a father cursed by
intoxicating drinks, who said himself that he had
seen but few days for nine years when he was free
from the power of strong drink. This daughter of
his seemed delighted with the new clothes and with
the Sunday-school and her teacher; but in a few
weeks she was taken ill (not dangerously), and I

learning the fact, called one stormy Sunday to see her, and was accompanied by my dear Brother Daniel Grokin, whose heart and hand, as well as that of his wife and children, was with us in this mission work. The tenement was in a building which had been used for a carpenter's shop, and but little alterations had been made to make it any way convenient for a residence (but it must be always remembered that poor drunkards are obliged to stay in many such places, while the persons who receive their hard earnings often live in fashionable and extravagant style). May God pity the women and children of the besotted drunkards of our land ! The little girl referred to was sitting in a chair as we entered the *staying-place* of this drunkard's family. We had taken with us some nice fruit and other articles suitable for the invalid girl, and made known the purpose of our visit to the father, who was then under the influence of strong drink. After a little conversation and the distribution of the goodies, we asked for the privilege of praying before we left. The father replied (not in a definite tone of voice) : " You can pray, if you like ; we are not used to that business here." We bowed before God, and earnestly besought His blessing upon the sick girl (who soon afterwards recovered), and upon the other children, and upon the mother and father also, and, before we left, the father and mother both promised to start in a new and better life; and ere the week closed, the heretofore inebriate father signed the Allen Mission total abstinence pledge, and he, with his wife, came to the altar, and by true repentance sought and found the pardon of their sins, and commenced a life of sobriety and religion. This brother for several years has taken care of the mission chapel, and has also been an active member in the Portland Reform Club, and its chaplain for several terms. As soon as he decided to be a total abstinence man, I procured for him work, so that he was enabled to procure food and raiment for his family. These reformed men need encouragement in many ways. May God impress upon His people this great responsibility in this direction. The conversion of these parents, and their increasing happiness consequent thereon, gave us new courage in our home mission work and from that time forward we had very much to cheer us—the numbers of attendants to our Sunday-school and other religious services constantly increasing, so it was thought best to have more frequent services; and in our work and visits among the poor and the outcasts, we were convinced more than ever before that the curse and evil of intemperance was producing more poverty and distress, degradation and sinfulness, than all other evils; and that God alone could give the needed wisdom and strength to help us in our efforts in "rescuing the perishing, and lifting up the fallen." We arranged a temperance pledge, to which in a few months we procured about four thousand signatures. The pledge was introduced into *all* our religious services as an important part. This temperance interest increasing, we deemed it best (and I have no doubt the thought came from our Master) to appoint a gospel temperance meeting, this being the first one of the kind we had ever heard of. There were doubts expressed by some of my dear brethren as to the feasibility of such a meeting; but believing fully that temperance was an important part of religion, we needed to look to God for help in this great work

It is evident that St. Paul considered temperance a part of the Gospel, when he preached to the Roman Governor about righteousness, *temperance*, and a judgment to come.

At our first gospel temperance prayer-meeting we had only *eight* persons in attendance; but the *ninth* was with us by His blessing and benediction. Those meetings in a few weeks became quite notorious in the community, and scores and hundreds came to them to sign the pledge, and many of them were found at the altar seeking the pardon and blessing of God. One evening as I was going to the Allen Mission Chapel to attend one of those Gospel Temperance Prayer Meetings, passing up the broad stairs to the entrance to the offices of the daily papers, my way was obstructed by a poor fallen one, who came tumbling down those stairs against me, and I soon found that he was under the influence of the demon of rum—a young man, the son of a godly mother, who was still living—and this young man also having a wife and child. As I raised him to his feet he recognized me as his friend; he having in his arms at the time a paper bag containing whiting which he used at his trade for cleaning silver ware, but in his fall, the bag was broken and the contents was spilled on the floor, and on himself and *myself also.* I took him to the door of a store near by and borrowed a brush-broom and so we made ourselves as free from the whiting as possible and I said to him, I wish you to go to the Mission, I am on my way there. In a few minutes he decided to go witn me. He was so debilitated by strong drink he could not well walk alone, and it was really with *much* difficulty, and after a full half-hour's trial and hard work, we arrived at the Mission, and the services were begun. During those services this young man knelt beside me, after signing the Total Abstinence Pledge, and asked God to help him to be a good man. The prayer was answered, and he very soon became an active worker in the Gospel Temperance Field—his wife and child and mother made happy, and this happiness continues. This young man is now a preacher of the Gospel and has a live Gospel Mission under his charge in a city in the State of Maine—to God be all the glory; and no doubt Brother P. often thinks of the long passage we had across the Lincoln Park, the night we crossed it, on our way to the Allen Mission when he signed the Pledge and resolved to be good. God will help us when we undertake to Lift up the Fallen.

CHAPTER II.

The gospel temperance meetings thus inaugurated in the Allen Mission have become one of the most efficient instrumentalities under God in helping forward the great gospel temperance reform movement, which, with God's blessing and under the leadership of Francis Murphy, is winning so many thousands of drunken men to sobriety and virtue. I will now, by the help and blessing of God, give an account of the wonderful conversion of Francis Murphy, which took place in the city of Portland, State of Maine, in the year 1870.

The work of the Allen Mission was not confined to the chapel and its services merely, but we were out among the poor and visiting the sick, and distributing food and clothing, as we had opportunity, and on these visits our own souls were greatly refreshed and comforted. In the midst of all the work and labor of love we have spoken of, our Master had other work for us, and in a direction which to many might not seem pleasant; but where the Lord leads it is always safe to follow.

In September, 1870, the sheriff or warden who had the oversight of our county jail, situated not

far from our mission chapel, came to me and desired to know if I was willing to conduct some religious services at the jail on the afternoon of each
Sabbath, he being convinced that such services
might result in good to the inmates; he desiring
me, also, to choose such associate brethren and sisters as I might deem best. After a little time for
reflection and consultation with those earnest co-
workers, I agreed to assume the responsibility, and
trust in God for results. During the intervening
week we took from our mission chapel a number of
settees, to be placed in the corridors of the jail for
the accommodation of the prisoners as they came
out of their cells to join with us in our worship;
and on the following Sabbath we were at the jail at
the hour appointed, 5 P. M.

Our number consisted of the writer and several
other Christian workers, both gentlemen and ladies
with hearts deeply imbued with the spirit of the
Master, who while He was upon earth went about
doing good. The outer and the inner doors of the
jail were open to us, and we were soon seated in close
proximity to the prisoners, who had left their cells
and occupied the settees sent from our Mission
chapel during the week. Our services were social
—reading of the Scriptures, prayer and song, with
short relations of Christian experience, and earnest
and warm-hearted appeals to the prisoners to seek

after the pardon and love of Christ. Near the close we presented the total abstinence pledge, and then gave the opportunity for any who desired to be prayed for, to manifest it by rising up. At this first service about one-third of the prisoners present (all the prisoners in the jail did not attend this service) arose and stood upon their feet, after which we all bowed in prayer, and the services were closed.

Coming out from the services, I passed near the front of a cell in which stood a man of excellent form and figure; but who looked sad and discouraged and apparently almost without hope. I could not pass him by carelessly, for I pitied him from my heart. I knew him and his history of trial and sorrow; I also knew the distressed situation of his family, and just then stepping up to the cell whose door was formed from iron bolts, I put my hands through between those iron bolts and bars, and took him by the hand (not by his fingers) and held on to it. Looking him in the face, I discovered tears starting from his eyes, and while brushing the tears from my own eyes, I said to him: " My dear brother, I pity you and wish you to become a Christian ; God will help you and we will help you ; will you attend the service with us next Sabbath ? "

He replied: " I have been a rum-seller and a rum-drinker, and have brought my wife and children into trouble and poverty, and I do not see how Christ can forgive me."

I replied: "Our Saviour came to seek and save just such persons as we are." He then said he would go into the service next Sabbath if I thought best ; and he added—Will you call and see my wife, and perhaps she will come and bring some of the children with her ? I told him I would call at his house as he desired, and bidding him cheer up, as there were better days for him, I left the prison.

During the early part of the week I called at the home of his wife and children, and gave them the message sent, and the reply I shall never forget: " I will do the best I can to be there, and perhaps bring some of the children." Oh! how I did wish just then to have some of the money that is spent for liquor, for I could have done so much good with it in helping this distressed family. Oh! that God would let His convicting power come upon the men of wealth, and show them what is their duty towards the distressed poor, and those ready to perish.

The next Sabbath found us at our post of duty. I usually spent the forenoon of each Sabbath visit- ing the sick and the poor and neglected, and pray- ing with them, and giving them advice and en- couragement as best I could ; frequently taking in hand some food and scrip, both of which were always gladly received. At 3 P. M. our Mission Sunday-school was gathered in the chapel, previous to which we held a prayer-meeting, continuing one hour. Closing the services at the chapel, we went to the jail to engage in the worship of God with the prisoners. The doors were opened to us, and as we were arranging to commence the services, the noise of little feet was heard along the corridor who were being led by their imprisoned father and their Christian mother and who were to be among the number of worshippers that day.

The father and mother occupied seats, but the children were so delighted to be with their papa once more, they sat in his lap or stood close by his side, and embraced and kissed him again and again, while tears filled the eyes of the mother, and of the prisoners, as well as of the Christian workers present. What cared the children for the prison if they could only be with their papa, from whom they had been separated, and who they loved so dearly. The little daughter who had been sitting by the side of her mother, had brought a bouquet of flowers which had been given her by a Christian friend ; and at length she took courage, stepped to the side of her father and presented him the flowers. After a little crying spell all around, the religious services commenced—reading the Scripture lesson—and songs and prayers were offered from warm and loving hearts and lips; then short Christian experiences were given, and loving and earnest appeals were made to the prisoners to accept the boon of Christ's pardon—the pearl of great price. The principle of supreme love to God, which would save and keep men from sin and from crime, and from jails and from prisons (as convicts), and make this present life happy, and give good hopes of a better life to come, was set forth, and near the close of the services the total abstinence pledge was signed by a large number of the prisoners, and then a cordial invitation was given by the leader (my humble self) to any who wished for the prayers of God's people present, that they might become Christians, and so lead better and happier lives, for all such to arise; and in one blessed minute nearly all of the prisoners arose to their feet, many of them bathed in tears. After a verse of that beautiful invitation hymn—

"Just as I am, without one plea,

we all bowed before God upon our knees, on the stone floor of that prison—prisoners (men and women), father, mother and children, and God's humble workers—and a prayer was offered first by the writer, and then other strong supplications from different brethren and sisters. Such appeals to God I never heard; and amid the tears and sighs of the poor penitents, and the prayers of faith that God would then and there convert these men and women to Himself, the power and love of the Saviour of poor sinners came down, and, breaking those stony hearts, put into their places hearts filled with light and joy and love; and among the number thus redeemed was Francis Murphy, whom God then and there chose to be His messenger, and from that eventful Sabbath service under God started the most glorious reform movement of the Nineteenth century. May He who thus favored this purely Gospel Temperance movement in its incipiency, and who has never left it without His approval, vouchsafe constantly His blessing and benediction and care over dear Brother Murphy and others of like precious faith who are laboring to help rescue the perishing and lift up the fallen.

The services soon closed, after the prisoners were urged to pray for themselves that evening in their cells at eight o'clock, which they promised to do; the Christian workers also agreeing to be found in prayer for them at the same time. Francis Murphy went into his cell, which seemed more light and pleasant than before; substantiating the truth of the poet that "With the presence of Christ prisons may palaces prove." The wife and mother, accompanied by her children, together with the Christian workers, all with thankful hearts and joyful lips, walked towards our homes, to tell the glad news of the redemption of the man who, under God, is now having such wonderful power and success in helping drinking men to sobriety and to Christ.

The next day (Monday) the news of the wonderful conversion at the county jail the day before was upon hundreds of lips. Some seemed to doubt it; others were hopeful and glad. Some said, "I don't believe that Frank Murphy is converted; he has only 'put it on' to get favors;" others said, "I don't believe in jail religion;" still others said, "This is one of Sturdivant's converts, and he won't stand six weeks before he will be found in the gutter, drunk, if they are fools enough to go his bail." I replied, if he were one of my converts, he would not stand six minutes before he would fall. Oh, what a spirit of distrust and doubt is found sometimes even among those of us who profess to be Christians! In our haste at the East we call such persons croakers; they don't seem to be willing to enter into the kingdom themselves, and are throwing hindrances in the way of the returning prodigal, as he turns his eyes and steps towards his Father's House.

I was accosted in the street and elsewhere to answer many questions, and to hear the different ideas and conclusions of the multitude. I was, however, so positive of the truth and reality of Francis Murphy's conversion, that I took the bold ground to

ask those inquirers if they had ever heard of Zaccheus, who one day was converted at his own house
while Christ the blessed Saviour was dining with him
and his family; or of St. Paul, who was once the
wicked Saul of Tarsus, but who was wondrously
converted by being struck blind for three days by a
ball of fire (of love) until he was willing to endure
all the persecutions of that age—had either of them
become apostates or backsliders?

They answered, "No."

I replied, "You will never hear of Francis Murphy backsliding, for the very same Jesus who won
Zaccheus and St. Paul and others of old to His service and work by giving them new hearts and as-
spirations, has won Francis Murphy." Very soon,
however, I am glad to say, nearly the whole community were fully convinced that Christ was able to
save to the uttermost—the one who had not only
suffered from the use of strong drink, but who had
for a time made a business of selling it to others.

Soon after the conversion of Mr. Murphy three
other gentlemen, with myself, desiring to have him
come out of his prison-home, and to be with his
family to support and comfort them, took the responsibility as sureties for his appearance at court
when wanted. Although we had no fears ourselves
but that Brother Murphy would be true and faithful,
I am sorry to say that others, who ought to have

had more charity, said : "Well, you will lose all the money you become responsible for. That Francis Murphy will soon be among the missing." Getting tired of such uncharitable talk, I said to them (perhaps too hastily) : "It was not your money we became responsible for, and it is none of your business."

This fact becoming known to Brother Murphy, he immediately wrote me a letter, in which he said : " Through your kindness and others, I am coming out of my prison-home to-day, and am to be permitted to see my dear wife and children, and to help care for them. I wish you to be at my house this evening, and to invite those brethren and sisters who have been so interested in me and my family, for I desire to *erect a family altar*." I read and re-read the letter, while tears of gratitude fell from my eyes. I soon personally gave the invitations, and also procured some grapes and other fruit to take to the children, as I desired they should have a good time.

At the time appointed we were at the house (new to him) of Brother Murphy. He, having arrived a short time before us, was delighted to see his friends, and so was his wife and children. Soon a suitable number of chairs for seats were borrowed from the neighbors, and we were all with one accord in one place—father and mother and children, and

Christian brethren and sisters. At the request of
Brother Murphy I took charge of the services.
We each read two verses from the Bible (the
best of all books), then a hymn was sung with
the spirit and with the understanding also; and
while songs of praise were ascending, tears from
the eyes of the joyful wife and children and
friends present, flowed thick and fast. Then
we all bowed before God, and prayers full of
expressed gratitude were offered by each adult
Then followed another hymn of praise, and then
short testimonies were given by each; the wife of
Brother Murphy making the closing one. With joy
beaming in her countenance, she stood up and said:
"This is the happiest hour of my life. I have been
praying to God for my husband for eleven years,
and He has heard my prayers, and converted his
soul, and I am the happiest woman living."

The grace of God is a precious boon; it gives
joy even in the midst of earthly poverty and want.
We soon distributed the fruit to the children and
others, and after singing " Praise God, from Whom
all blessings flow," and bidding each a good-night,
we returned to our homes with light hearts, and no
headache.

In a few weeks after this glad evening Sister Murphy was taken ill with symptoms of fever. Brother
Murphy, desiring to see me, I was soon with him,

and after consultation, the services of an excellent physician, Dr. True, were secured, and in a few days high hopes were entertained of her recovery ; but in a day or two Brother Murphy desired to see me again, sending word that his dear wife was not so well, and asked me to come and pray with them. Before engaging in prayer, I asked Sister Murphy what she desired we should pray for. She replied: " God has given me a new husband ; life *now* seems more desirable, and if it is God's will I would like to live: and what will these six little children do without their mother ?"

Brother Murphy, myself and the children bowed before God, in the room where this saint of His lay ill, and asked with submission for her recovery to health. Friends from the Allen Mission and others did all they could to help care for the children, and to make comfortable as possible the sick wife and mother.; but it seems her Heavenly Father thought it best to take her to His rest in Heaven. She was soon convinced of this, but she was not afraid—it was her Father who was leading her; yet it is a terrible struggle for mothers to give up their children, especially young children, and to leave them in this cold, unfriendly world. The struggle with her would have been more severe, only for the fact that she was to leave the children in the care of their new Christian and loving father. In this eventful hour the husband received the last kiss from his devoted and loving and patient wife; and the children also, one by one, came to the bed-side to kiss their mamma for the last time, and also to receive advice from their dying mother, such as alone can be given under similar circumstances. Then she was ready, and the angels from the better land soon appeared to convey her weary spirit home to the heavenly rest. I was at once sent for by dear Brother Murphy, and was in a few moments by his side. He was broken-hearted, and I pitied him from my inmost soul. Said he: "What shall I do, Brother Sturdivant? She's gone!"

I told him we must not murmur nor complain, but trust in God, who doeth all things well.

After a little season of mutual, heartfelt sympathy, Brother Murphy said: " Brother Sturdivant, I have no place where to bury my dear wife, and nothing to meet the expenses." I replied, " I know it—she shall have a Christian funeral, and a Christian burial, and the Mission will see to it all;" and God enabled us to fulfill the promises made. I will here and now say (and my readers must not think me egotistical), that if it had taken the last dollar I had on earth, I would cheerfully have given it to Brother Murphy in his affliction and distress.

The funeral services took place in a few days, and the earthly remains of Sister Murphy were taken to the beautiful Evergreen Cemetery, followed by the deeply afflicted husband and children, and the writer and other Christian friends, there to remain until the resurrection of the just.

Of Brother Murphy's early life, and of his life since his conversion, with all of its intensely interesting, and touching, and useful events and incidents, he himself has given to the world.

BEHIND THE PRISON BARS.

CHAPTER III.

SCENES IN MISSION AND PRISON WORK.

Now, leaving (not forgetting—no, never!) the one who has occupied our thoughts for awhile, I will proceed to give accounts of other interesting conversions and incidents in connection with our Allen

43

Mission work, among the poor, and the outcast, and the inebriates, and the prisoners.

My readers will please remember that for more than six years I had the care and oversight of the religious services at the county jail in Portland, which labor I did cheerfully and without any reward from men, but from a feeling given me by God for poor, fallen humanity, and this service was in addition to the work at the Chapel, and other outside work; but I had, all these years, good and tried Christian associate workers, both men and women —God bless them! I only wish I could give to the world the full history of their loving words and deeds. But their names and works and deeds are written in the Lamb's book of life, and "They shall be Mine on that day when I make up my jewels, saith the Most High and Holy One."

Soon after the war of the Rebellion, many strangers came to our city, some of whom were profligate and intemperate young men. Looking in the morning papers one day, I noticed the fact of the arrest of three young men, who, while on a drunken spree, and in order to get money to procure more liquor, broke into a store and took therefrom articles to the amount of about thirty dollars in value. They were brought to Court, tried and found guilty. One of these young men had been in State's prison before, and his sentence was more severe; he was sentenced to State's prison for ten years, while the other two (this being their first offence against the law) were sent to prison for five years each. While waiting for trial and sentence in the county jail, those three young men resolved to lead good lives in the future; and one of them, by his good behavior, had his sentence shortened from five to four years. He left the prison with a good name from the Warden; and when last heard from by the writer was living a good life.

The young man who was sentenced for a term of ten years has been good and true, and his term will be shortened, and he will soon be out, to show to the world, I trust, that the grace of God, sought and found in prison, is able to save and to keep.

The other young man, whose history I feel to be more particular in giving, was sentenced to six years' hard labor in State's prison. Before leaving the county jail, to go to the State's prison at Thomaston, Maine, he expressed a desire that I would correspond with him, which I readily promised to do; impressing on his mind the importance of his being faithful and obedient to the officers of the prison, as well as to his God. I soon wrote him a letter, and in a few days received an answer; and my heart was cheered on receiving this, his first letter to me, as it gave good evidence of his conversion and true piety. Our correspondence was faithfully kept up, week by week, I feeling more than an ordinary interest in this young man, he having no father or mother, or sister or brother to care for him. His home, before the war, was at Savannah, Ga., at which city he enlisted in the rebel army, at the outbreak of the rebellion. He was captured and made prisoner by the Union army, and after his release he enlisted in the Union service, and shipped on board one of our naval ships; but finding the wound he received while in battle made it extremely hard to do the duties assigned him, he left the sea service and came on shore, and, following the use of strong drinks, which habit he had formed while in the army, was arrested as before stated.

In my letters to this young Christian brother I would not only give him the best counsel and advice I was capable of, but would often enclose small sums of money, that he might be able to purchase articles of comfort and convenience, as he was allowed to do by the kind officials of the prison. By the spirit of his letters I could discover an apparent growth in grace and spirituality, accompanied with increased contentment and true Christian reconciliation to his circumstances, also, an expressed desire to be useful to the world when he should again be out in it. I asked him if he did not feel that God had some *special* work for him to do, and he replying in the affirmative, we thought best to send him such books as would enable him to procure a preparation for a life of usefulness in the vineyard of the Lord. I will confess to a little selfishness, for I did so strongly desire, after his prison-life terminated, he might become a help to me and my associate workers at the Allen Mission.

I visited him at the prison, in a few months after his entering that institution, and he was delighted to see me. Our correspondence continued for nearly two years; but about this time I discovered his letters came less frequent, and I felt an anxiety, fearing for the moment that in some hour of temptation he might have neglected the *important* Christian duty of secret prayer, and thereby have back-slidden from God.

However, I soon received a letter from the Warden (Mr. W. W. Rice, whom no man ever excelled in real adaptation, in all respects, to the difficult and responsible position which he occupied, and still holds), saying my friend Sheldon was ill and had been out of the workshop, and in the hospital department of the prison, for several weeks, and that his symptoms were consumptive; but he (the Warden) said it was his opinion he might be restored if he could be taken out of prison and properly nursed and cared for; in the same communication intimating if I would take the responsibility, he would procure a pardon from the Governor.

I immediately made known the contents of the letter to my associate workers at the Allen Mission, and although we were not in possession of but little money, yet, as we had been reading Sheldon's letters from time to time, in our public services at the Mission, and praying for him, and were truly and earnestly interested in him, we decided at once that the poor motherless and fatherless young man should not die in prison, and we had hope that God might restore him to health, if he could be under our care.

The next day one of my associate workers, Brother Daniel Gookin, took the cars for Thomaston, to bring the sick young Brother Sheldon to Portland, where we could properly care for him. I at once proceeded to procure a boarding place, and also a nurse, to help to take good care of our sick prison Brother on his arrival, and the Christian women of our Mission (God bless them!) made comfortable and pleasant arrangements for his reception, as though it was their own brother. So, for the time being, and until his death, these Christian women never relaxed their efforts for his happiness. Brother Gookin, arriving at Thomaston late in the evening, visited Sheldon in his sick room; Sheldon's first inquiry was:

" Where is Brother Sturdivant?"

Brother Gookin replied, " He could not come to

see you, but has sent me to bring you to Portland."

The message overcame the dear sick prison Brother, and he replied, " I am so ill, I fear I cannot
survive to reach Portland, and, besides, they will
not let me out of prison."

Brother Gookin assured him the Governor would
permit him to leave. He slept but little that night;
the prospect and hope of not dying in the prison made
him glad and wakeful. In the morning he was better, elated and happy. His prison clothes were ex-
changed for a citizen's suit, together with a new pair
of boots, and a five-dollar bill in his pocket—all the
gifts of Warden Rice. Sheldon left his sick room,
and, with the help of Brother Gookin, he was enabled to endure the ride of seventy-five miles to
Portland in the cars. I was at the depot with a carriage to receive him, and to take him to his new
home. He was so overjoyed to see me that tears
came thick and fast over his pale and emaciated
face. Arriving at the boarding place, he was received by the Christian women of the Allen Mission
and refreshed with little delicacies, provided by
loving hearts and willing hands, acting as angels of
mercy, taking the places of his own mother and sister.

Sheldon, in a short time, by this kind treatment
and nursing, and the advice of an excellent physician (Dr. True, God bless him! he is so kind and

benevolent to the poor, and for all the weeks he attended this sick brother from the prison he did not charge one cent), he began to show symptoms of improvement, which lasted, however, only a few days. Soon after this, his cough became more severe and hard, so much so that it disturbed the other boarders in the house, and this fact was made known to me by the landlady desiring me to procure another boarding place for the sick young man. This was a new trial for me and for others who loved this Brother so well. I at once, with a heart trusting in God, made the effort, and very unexpectedly met, upon the street, one of our Mission workers, and made known to her that I was in pursuit of a new boarding place for Sheldon. She replied, "We can take him at our house." I expressed my gratification, and I agreed to procure a nurse to take care of the sick brother. The reply was, "Husband and I will do that, and we will give up our *best room* also, for the poor, sick, motherless young man." This was said by the wife of a sea-captain—noble-hearted woman, and man, who under their existing circumstances would offer to do this. We removed Brother Sheldon to his new home, and he was made so comfortable and had such good attendance and nursing, that for several days he seemed much better; but it was only the apparent and flattering improvement of a consumptive.

Our Mission workers would often gather in the room where the sick man lay, and evening after evening hold social prayer meetings, in which Brother Sheldon was deeply interested, and which services seemed to strengthen even his body and to comfort his mind. After a few weeks he grew more and more ill; and, with all that human skill and kindness could do, it was evident that his disease would very soon end in death. On several occa·sions during the few last weeks of his life, he would send especially for me, thinking himself to be dying, wishing me to be with him in that solemn hour. I would cheerfully hasten to his bedside, and sing and pray with him, and he would be glad and revive again, and be better for awhile.

Early one morning I was sent for, with the in-formation that he was dying and wished to see me. I hastened at once to his bedside, but his spirit had gone to the land of rest, where his mother and father had gone, and where there are no more pris-ons nor death. In two days after his death we took the frail, worn and weary body of our prison Brother to the Mission Chapel, where appropriate funeral services were held, and although no mother, nor father, nor sister, nor brother were there to shed tears of sympathy and sorrow, yet hundreds of true mourners, with sad hearts and tearful eyes were in that congregation, giving expressions of tenderness and love towards the dead young Brother whom the Mission workers were not willing should die in prison; and these loving friends followed his earthly remains to our Allen Mission lot, where we tenderly deposited them, to remain until the earth and the sea give up their dead.

"I was sick and in prison and ye came unto me," were the words of our Saviour; and if we follow His teachings, we shall be willing, yea, esteem it a privilege to obey, even though it leads us to jails and State prisons, to try and help the inmates to become the followers of our Master and Redeemer.

About this time we found a man among the inmates of our jail—a man by name of Plunkett—who had been committed for abusing his wife, while under the influence of intoxicating drink, and he having become so abusive, it was thought best, for the real safety of his wife and children, thus to commit him for the term of sixty days. He came into our religious services on Sabbath afternoon, and was struck under conviction, on account of his sins, bowed his will to the will of Christ, and was truly converted to God. He remained in jail for several weeks after his conversion, and took part in the religious exercises, and gave good evidence of a real change of heart. After having served out his time in the jail he returned to his home, erected at once a family altar (I would recommend that all

reformed men who have families go and do like-
wise), and took his children to Sunday-school and
to church, and soon became a member of the
church, taking active part in all church work. He
put glass in the window frames, where old hats and
rags had poorly supplied its place; put new hinges
on the doors of the barn and other buildings; and
the yard in front of his house was re-fenced, and
the general appearance of his house was wonderfully improved, the former *staying* place of the
drunkard became the happy *home* of the Christian,
and the fearful wife and children became the happy
inmates of a God-renovated *house*.

HAPPY HOME.

Brother Plunkett soon entered upon the work of
speaking for humanity and for Christ, and became,
and is now, a very effective and, I may truly say,

eloquent speaker and worker in the Gospel Temperance field; thus showing additional evidences of the power of the Gospel to save from intemperance and sin.

Among the prisoners at the county jail who found his way there through the terrible effects of intemperance, was a young man of more than ordinary ability. He had a beautiful and accomplished wife and a sweet little daughter, four years of age. But the habit of using strong drink had fastened upon him its terrible grasp, and made him abusive and cruel to her he promised to love, cherish and protect. So cruel he became that his wife's father took her and her little daughter to his own home; but while this young man was paying his penalty for transgressing the law, by being confined in the county jail, he was influenced to sign the total abstinence pledge, and became a better man, and after coming out from his prison, he lived such a correct life that his wife consented to live with him again. Our Mission helped them to start anew in housekeeping; and, accordingly, one evening, made them a surprise call, and took with us articles of furniture, and other things useful in houskeeping; and the occasion was one of real pleasure to the givers as well as the recipients, for the good Book says, "It is more blessed to give than to receive."

One other young man was in the jail for the theft

of a yoke of oxen. He was only a *moderate drinker*, but it took all his spare money to maintain this habit. He had fallen in love with a young lady; and so wished to make her some valuable present, as proof of his esteem, and, having no money, and with brain turned to bad, no doubt by strong drink, he took a neighbor's yoke of very valuable oxen and sold them to obtain money to purchase the desired presents, but he was arrested and put into jail. After being incarcerated in prison awhile, as his father thought long enough to punish him sufficiently, he was released by his kind-hearted father, who paid the bill for the stolen oxen and other accrued expenses. This young man, while in jail, signed the total abstinence pledge and became a converted man. My advice would be to young ladies who are waited upon by wayward young men, not to accept any valuable presents from them, unless they are sure the money purchasing said presents was not obtained from sale of stolen oxen.

It would take a large book to contain an account of the many interesting incidents and facts arising from, and connected, with, our work among the prisoners at the county jail for more than six years.

I must now return to some facts and incidents connected with our work at the Allen Mission Chapel, among the children, and others who came to our religious services. One evening, at an early hour, a woman, who often came to the Mission, called at my house, and desired me to come to her *staying place* (for she had a drunken husband—and I contend there is no *home* where the drunkard is; for home means peace, and love, and happiness), to see if I could not persuade him to sign the pledge of total abstinence, and to bring the pledge with me (it is very essential to have some blank pledges about your person always), for, she said, " I think he will sign it for you. He has been abusing me (showing at the same time the evident marks of abuse on her arms), and nearly ruined what little furniture I had." I made the visit that evening, and found the man under the influence of strong drink, and also with him a friend, as he called him, who was also under the influence of the demon rum.

After awhile they became more quiet, and both signed the pledge, and we bowed before God in prayer; and one of them also prayed for himself, and soon became a converted man, and became one of the Mission workers. The other is keeping his pledge, but has not, to my knowledge, become a Christian man. I could well have made excuse not to have made the call that evening, but could not feel right to deny the expressed wish of the drunkard's wife. When I consider the suffering and sorrow and heart-ache and agony and distress of thousands and tens of thousands of women and children of our country, occasioned and experienced through the use of intoxicating liquors by fathers and husbands and sons, I cannot see any other way for me but to give my whole energies, and time, and life to help rescue and save those unfortunate men.

"MIGHTY GLAD TO DIE!"

One day I was riding in my carriage near the suburbs of the city, and when near to a cross-road that led to and from a shipyard, I discovered two small girls coming toward me, each with a basket of wood and chips which they had gathered, to take to their homes for fuel. One of the girls belonged to our Mission, a very bright and intelligent Scotch girl, whose father was a drunkard. I took both of the children into my carriage, with the two baskets of wood, and continued my pleasant ride to the city, for it has always been a real pleasure for me to give the poor children a ride in my carriage. The little Scotch girl's mother had been ill for a long time; consequently, my first inquiry of Rosa was:

"How is your mother, to-day?"

Looking me sorrowfully in the face, she quickly replied:

"Mother is dead, and was buried yesterday."

I said: "You surprise me; how did she feel about dying, Rosa?"

"She replied: "Oh, she was *mighty glad to die!*"

"Well, what did she say about leaving you, Rosa?"

"Mother said the Lord would take care of me."

Oh, there are wives and mothers of drunken husbands and sons, all over the land, who are feeling in their inmost souls they would be *mighty glad to die*; they do not often *say* much about it, but they feel it. May God, in mercy, arouse His people to buckle on their whole armor, and go forth to battle against this terrible enemy of mankind—strong drink—which is filling our jails, and prisons, and penitentiaries, and lunatic asylums with seven-eighths of all their inmates, and sending to the drunkard's grave and to darkness one man or woman in every twenty minutes of time; and so leaving thousands and tens of thousands of orphan children to struggle along life's journey as best they can, with the help of the cold charity of the world.

But a brighter day is dawning, thank God; men and women are being redeemed from this terrible vice, and are becoming wonderful instruments for the uplifting of other fallen ones, and also men and women who have never suffered *personally*, are beginning to feel that God has a work for them to do in this part of His vineyard.

To show that the latter class are thus being influenced by our gracious Master, I will give th facts in regard to one among the many, and who has been a useful, and efficient, and earnest worker in the Gospel Temperance field for the last few years, at the Allen Mission, and in and out of the city, wherever he may, in the. Providence of God be called.

He has been one of my steamboat friends and associates for more than twenty-five years; and is still admitted to be the leading steamboat man in New England. I refer to Captain J. B. Coyle, who, three years ago last August, at the old Orchard National Gospel Temperance Camp-meeting, gave his new experience in nearly the following language. Rising at the front of the platform on the preacher's stand, surrounded by a large number of ministers and laymen, and facing a vast audience of more than five thousand people, he said :

"Christian brethren and friends, in October last as I was rising from my bed, the sun just throwing its early morning rays into my chamber, I heard what seemed to me an audible voice, say :

"Do you know that you are more than sixty years

" I answered ' I did not realize it."

" ' And what have you done' " ?

" I anwered, ' I have done nothing, Lord ; what wilt thou have me to do ?' "

" ' Get you up, and go into the city (Captain Coyle's residence is one mile out of the city), and you will meet a man and he will tell you what to do ?' "

" I went into the city that morning, and met on the street my old friend, Brother Sturdivant, who spoke to me, and asked me to come to the Alien Mission, and speak that night in the Gospel Temperance meeting. He said there was a great interest there, and he wished me to help him I replied that I could not talk in public. He said, ' You come to-night and try ; ' but I would not promise him fully about the matter then. At noon I went to my home, and told my wife Brother Sturdivant desires me to be at the Allen Mission to-night and make a speech, would you go, wife?' ' Yes,' she replied, ' you ought to go and help him.' "

" After dinner I went into the city again, and was riding through the streets, and who should I meet again but this same Brother Sturdivant, who asked me again to be present that evening at the Allen Mission. I gave him to understand I would be present, but he must not expect me to speak."

" Evening came, and I went into the city, but did

not go near the Allen Mission Chapel until I was well assured the services were begun. Arriving at the door, I could not have courage to enter, but walked back and forth in front of the entrance, just as an old toper does in front of a drinking saloon when he has no money. After awhile I mustered courage and entered the chapel, which was filled with worshipers, and Brother Sturdivant saw me at once, and beckoned me to come forward and sit with him within the altar rail. Walking tremblingly up the aisle, one of the mottoes of evergreen on the clear white walls of the chapel arrested my attention, for it read: 'God is Love.' Yes, thought I, and He has loved and cared for me all these years. This thought softened my poor heart, and from that time to this I have been more happy than heretofore, and, if more useful, I owe it all to the instrumentality of Brother Sturdivant for his invitation to go to the Allen Mission and to help him in the Gospel Temperance meetings.

"I was called upon by Brother Sturdivant during the evening to make a speech; and I arose tremblingly and gave my testimony in favor of the Gospel Temperance movement, whose moral power is inducing such numbers to give up the terrible habit of drinking intoxicating liquors, which power and truth I saw on the walls of the Allen Mission, in those blessed words, 'God is Love.'"

There are thousands of good and true men, in and out of the Church of Christ, who might accomplish a vast amount of good in this great field of Gospel Temperance, if they would only realize the blessed truth that "God is Love." With this powerful weapon, in the name of our Great Leader, let the women and men and children of the land go forth to fight the enemy of humanity—Intoxicating Drink—and He will, ere long, give the victory; and may those thousands who are hearing the voice of God saying to them, "What hast thou done?" reply, as did the noble-hearted steamboat captain, "Lord, what wilt Thou have me to do?"

In thinking over the work of the Allen Mission, incident after incident and fact after fact come so fresh and vivid to my mind, that I often imagine myself among the poor children in the Sunday-school, so happy and ready to receive the instruction given, or in the sewing-room of the Circle, waiting anxiously, although patiently, to have fitted for them some new clothes or shoes, with which they always seemed so delighted. The children, many of them, will ere long become men and women, good and true and faithful and useful citizens; others have gone on early to the bright and beautiful land above.

One of the girls who attended the Mission for years lost her loving father by death—and his wife, being left with several children to support, had to struggle hard against poverty. The girl I speak of was one on whom her mother had fond hopes of help; but she was stricken down suddenly and died, before I knew even of her sickness. One noonday a man stepped into my office, and said the dear girl living on Poplar street, who thought so much of you, is dead, and to be buried this afternoon at 3 o'clock (it was then nearly one), and her mother wishes you to be present. Of course I would go, if possible. I went to this house of mourning, although in the midst of pressing business, and found a few neighbors and friends present, for the house was very small, and the poor have but *few* friends. May our rich Heavenly Father in mercy help the poor.

We waited and waited, as I supposed, for the minister to make his appearance; I then learned that no minister of the Gospel had been even asked to be present. I took the Bible and read words of consolation from its pages, and then offered prayer to the God of the poor, that His blessing might be given to the stricken mother and the little brothers and sisters. After those simple services were closed, the remains of this poor, fatherless girl were borne to her resting-place, followed by only *one* carriage. I am thankful that Christ has said He is preparing many mansions, so I have faith to believe that the poor, homeless and houseless girls and boys of the land will have as good a home in Heaven as the rich of earth.

Another one of our mission girls, only eleven years of age, took sick with the dropsy (a disease not common among young children in New England), and after a few months she died in great peace—fell asleep in the arms of the Saviour, who, while He was upon earth, said, "Suffer little children to come unto me, and forbid them not."

Her father was drowned in the Atlantic Ocean, and her mother came from the British Provinces to procure employment, with the hope of educating her children. This daughter came to our Sunday-school, and was a little favorite. She was a good singer, and would recite very interesting prose and poetry at the Mission Sunday-school concerts, and she was a real comfort to her mother. But God thought best to take her where her father had gone —to the country that St. John in the Revelation saw, "where there was no more sea." I frequently visited her during her illness; she could not lie down, although very sick, but her mother would do all she could to "bolster her up." I learned from this dear little girl lessons of Christian faith and resignation such as I seldom have learned elsewhere. While ill she would constantly be at work making little worsted mats to be sent to the Mission fairs and festivals, to be sold for some trifling sum of money, to help her mother purchase bread. As I would enter the room where she was ill, and approaching her, would say :

"Gertrude, how is it with you, to-day ?" Her reply was quickly given :

"I am nicely; all ready, waiting for the Saviour to come."

Calling one day to see her, I found the Saviour had come and taken her, and during a cold snow-storm her once distressed and worn body was taken to the resting place of the dead, and her youthful and happy spirit had flown to the country where the inhabitants say "I am never sick."

I sometimes think, amid my trials and disappointments and conflicts, how blessed it will be to see those dear children again ; and if I am so blessed as to gain the golden stairway that leads to the gate of the New Jerusalem, I shall find those dear Mission children, as well as others who have passed on before, waiting and watching for me.

Thus I have endeavored, in my plain way, to give a few of the many facts and incidents in connection with my home mission work in which I have been so deeply interested for more than fifteen years past; and have been doing all I could with the limited means at my disposal to help feed the hungry and to clothe the naked, and also to visit the sick, and the men and women in the jails and prisons of the land, and to try and persuade men to give up the intoxicating cup, sign the temperance pledge and come to Christ and be saved.

CHAPTER IV.

I am glad to be able to say before God that I have done the best I could in these directions with the time I could spare from my business hours; and my business has been such as to absorb nearly my whole time during the day for the last twelve years, I having been an associate agent and general agent of a steamboat line, whose steamers ply along the eastern coast of Maine. In this business I continued until January, 1877, when a change in the company took place, and I thought it my imperative duty then and henceforth to give up all my time, and the remainder of my life to the Gospel Temperance work; and I was the more fully convinced when I found my little property had all gone, and I was left without one dollar to help my family or myself.

About this time I received a letter from Brother Francis Murphy, who was just opening up the great work of Gospel Temperance in Philadelphia, desiring me to come to Philadelphia and help. As soon as I could arrange my business matters, I left Portland for Philadelphia, the month of May, 1877.

Arriving in Philadelphia I was very gladly received by Brother Murphy, made my home with him, and at once commenced to devote my whole time to do what I could to help forward the gracious work of reform then going on among the drinking men and women. The meetings increased in interest and in numbers, and nearly one hundred thousand persons signed the Murphy Total Abstinence Pledge, during the meetings held in Concert Hall and in the Annex building, and in the different churches in the city; and the results of those efforts of Brother Murphy's and other faithful workers, both ministers and laymen, women and men, will only be known in eternity.

After working for the Master in Philadelphia and vicinity for about five weeks, it was thought advisable for me to visit Pittsburgh, I having frequent invitations. I had formed many pleasant and valuable acquaintances in the City of Brotherly Love, during my stay of five weeks. Some of them I have seen since my return, and others have passed on to the better land. I have also been much pleased to learn, from good authority, that nearly eighty per cent. of the men who were reformed, during the Murphy meeting of last year, have kept the pledge, and very many have connected themselves with the different churches in the city.

One incident occurred before leaving for Pittsburgh which I wish to relate, to show that we have joyful occasions as well as seasons of sadness in our work, and to show how grateful even children are when their fathers give up the drinking of intoxicating liquors and become Christians. One morning a drinking man left his home in Camden, N. J., to come to Philadelphia to seek employment. His wife had been dead for some years, his daughter living at home, and as her father left the house she said to him:

"Pa, I hope you won't come home intoxicated to-night."

The father came across the ferry. The message of his dear little daughter had been fastened to his soul. He called at several places, asking for employment, and was nnsuccessful. He thought to himself he would try for employment in a drinking saloon, as years previous he had been a bartender. Here he received an offer, the man giving him ten dollars in advance, and he was to commence his services the next day. He had a friend and old comrade in the Post-office, whom he called to see, to ask advice about accepting the offer to tend bar. That friend (Captain W. A. Leaborn, who is now one of the most successful Gospel Temperance advocates in town) had gone to the Murphy meeting at the Annex. The Camden man went to the Annex meeting, and hearing Brother Murphy and others talking about the joys of total abstinence, and the power of God's grace to save and to keep, went forward with others and took the pledge.

That evening the man returned to his home, and on his way called at the saloon and told the barkeeper he had signed the total abstinence pledge, and could not serve him, handing him at the same time the ten dollars which was advanced to him in the morning. Arriving at his home, he was met by his affectionate daughter, who asked him if he had procured any employment, and answered, "No daughter; but I have got something better—I have the pledge (showing it at the same time), and have signed it, and by God's help I will never break it."

SIGNING THE PLEDGE.

The motherless girl expressed her joy as best she could, while her father told her of his eventful visit to the Murphy temperance meeting, and said, "I saw Mr. Murphy and shook hands with him, and I also saw the man who, under God, encouraged Mr. Murphy to start in his new life." The little daughter replied: "I would like to see that wonderful man, Mr. Murphy, and also the man who befriended him." Her father was at the Annex meeting the next day, and said to me: "My *little* daughter would like very much to see Brother Murphy and yourself (she has no clothes suitable to come over here to meeting at present), she wants to give you a kiss." Brother Murphy's duties kept him so closely at the Annex Meetings, he could not leave; but as it had been already announced for me to speak at Camden, I told the father I would be at the church early, and would be glad to see his *little* daughter and receive the proffered kiss.

Arriving at the church in good season, I found the father, with his *little* daughter by his side, ready for an introduction to me, and before the introduction was fairly finished, I received a warm kiss upon my lips, not from a little girl of six years, as I supposed her previously to be, but from a young lady of eighteen summers, who thus expressed her gratitude to God for having given me existence, as she said, to be the means of helping Francis Murphy to a better life under God, and he influencing her dear father to become a good man. This reformed man at once entered the Gospel Temperance field as a speaker and laborer, and is still doing good service for poor fallen humanity. Week before last I saw him at the Camden ferry, and gave him an invitation to come to Eighth Street Church, above Buttonwood, where we have been holding Gospel Temperance meetings on the Murphy plan for more than six weeks. He readily accepted the invitation, and gave us one of the most powerful speeches of all the hundreds we have been blessed with. To God be all the Glory.

Almost every day during the protracted Gospel Temperance meetings at the Annex, touching and very interesting incidents and facts occurred, proving that the power of love and the practice of the motto —"With malice towards none and charity for all," is accomplishing wonders through the instrumentality of the men and women whom God is redeeming from the thraldom of strong drink, and sending them forth in His vineyard to labor.

Soon after this I left for Pittsburgh, and arriving there, I found glad hearts and warm hands among the officers of the National Christian Temperance Union, and the ladies of the Old Home Guard and others. They soon planned work for me, and arranged for union services in the different churches in Pittsburgh and Allegheny City. Those meetings, as well as the noonday prayer meetings at the "Old Home," were occasions of the manifest power of God's grace and mercy in redeeming and saving men from the love of strong drink.

During these series of meetings, a man, who had been separated from his wife for several years —they both being in the habit of drinking to excess —came forward and signed the total abstinence pledge. He soon began to respect himself and realize that he had some manhood left, and becoming more strong in his will to keep the pledge, and also convinced his help must come from God. He thought of his wife, and told me a few days after his conversion that he would find her, if possible, and persuade her to come to the meetings and sign the pledge. One evening soon after, as I was about among the audience, inviting persons to come forward and sign the pledge, I discovered this man, and speaking to him, asked if his wife was present. He replied, "Yes, this is her." I being introduced, asked her if she would step forward and sign the pledge (she showed convincing marks of dissipation). After hesitating a moment, she with her husband and myself, standing in front of the table on which lay the pledges, tremblingly took the pen and affixed her name to the pledge. I then said to them: "Is it your desire and determination, each of you, by God's help, to keep these vows as long as you live; and do you also desire to live together again as man and wife? if so, please join hands." I will assure you they were not long in joining hands, and I hope hearts also, and we bowed at once before Almighty God and asked Him to seal these vows thus made in the presence of His people, and to keep them both unto the end of life free from the curse of strong drink. During those short services hundreds of handkerchiefs in the congregation were in use arresting the falling tears.

After a few weeks of this Gospel Temperance work in Pittsburgh and vicinity, Mr. J. K. Barber, Secretary of the National Christian Temperance Union, made arrangements for me to speak at several cities in the oil regions. Those appointments I filled to the best of my ability, and the people seemed very glad to see me and to hear me, and treated me very kindly, indeed. I trust my visit to the cities of Parker, Franklin, Titusville and Oil City resulted in good to many.

Returning to Pittsburgh and spending a few days, I did what I could to help along the reform work. Soon after my return from the oil regions, arrangements were made for me to speak at Columbus, Ohio. After bidding the good people of Pittsburgh good-bye (whose kindness to me I shall never forget), I left for Columbus, where I remained several

days and gave several addresses to the people of
that beautiful city, the former home of President
Hayes and his estimable wife, (God bless her!) who
had moral courage and strength enough to remove
the wine-cup from the dinner table at the White
House.

The Sabbath I was in Columbus I was invited by
Brother Ogden to attend religious services at the
State Penitentiary, which service occurred during
the forenoon. I was introduced to Brother Wil-
liams, the chaplain, the right man in the right place,
and he desired me to address the prisoners. On
going into the large chapel I was surprised to see
such a vast audience before me, numbering sixteen
hundred (as I was informed), all dressed in prison
uniform. May God save the boys, now coming to
manhood, from the curse of strong drink, and from
the disgrace of wearing a prison uniform. In this
place the uniform was woolen, white and black
striped. Besides the prisoners present, about four
hundred citizens, men and women, were seated in
the gallery of the chapel, making in all about two
thousand persons—and I to speak to such a vast
audience! The Lord did, in great mercy, help me,
so that I was enabled to talk to them about thirty
minutes, the time allotted; and seeing so many of
the prisoners shed tears, it drew upon my sympa-
thies very strongly indeed. I may never see many

of those men again, but hope, when their term of imprisonment expires, they will never be found in prison again as transgressors of the law.

After remaining a few days at Columbus, I was invited to attend a Gospel Temperance tabernacle meeting in the grove, under a large tent, at Urbana, the meeting proving under God a wonderful success, large numbers signing the total abstinence pledge, and coming to the altar to seek God's pardon and grace. At this interesting meeting I formed many valuable acquaintances. Among the number were several of those women of God who had the moral courage, a few years since, to start out in the great and glorious crusade movement in the West. They are still in the Gospel Temperance work, and rejoicing also in what God is now doing in rescuing poor fallen humanity—both men and women—from the curse and slavery of strong drink.

From Urbana, on invitation, I visited the towns and cities of Springfield, Harrisville, London, Eaton, Piqua, Seven Mile, Xenia and Dayton, all in the State of Ohio; also the city of Richmond, and several towns in Indiana, at all of which towns and cities very interesting meetings were held, and the Gospel Temperance work on the Murphy plan under God was accomplishing wonderful good.

In the city of Indiana, of fifteen thousand inhabitants, during the temperance revival of twelve weeks the public sale of strong drink was reduced eighty-five per cent., and nearly all the liquor saloons in that city were closed for want of custom.

In all of the towns and cities I visited, I was cordially received and kindly treated, and formed valuable acquaintances which I shall never forget.

While at Dayton, Ohio, the meetings were of more than ordinary interest, and the excitement was so great and universal that several meetings were held each night in the largest halls and churches in the city. The first evening of my arrival at Dayton I spoke in a large hall to a crowded audience, and I had wonderful freedom; I can only account for it from the fact that beside me, on the platform, where I stood to speak, was one of God's noble women—a woman of faith and earnest prayer, although so afflicted in body that for more than fourteen years she had not been able to walk or stand, but was obliged to lie in a reclining posture. On that evening she was brought to the meeting by her brother upon a carriage-bed; this carriage was upon the platform near me, and as I was speaking I turned my eyes, and beholding her patient and resigned look and heavenly-inspired and interested countenance, I had such an inspiration come to my help as I never before realized. I refer to Miss Jennie Smith, of Dayton, Ohio, who has given to the world that wonderfully interesting book, "The

Valley of Baca—a record of Suffering and Triumph."

This most excellent Christian lady, feeling an intense desire that she might be restored so as to be able to walk, decided to try the skill and treatment to be found at Cuthbert Street Hospital, Philadelphia. The experiment, by God's blessing, has secured to her the desire of her heart, and she is now restored, and able to walk, and to work still more effectually to help poor fallen humanity to better lives.

While in Dayton I was invited to visit Cincinnati. I spoke in this queen city of the West for about ten days during the early part of July, and although the weather was extremely warm, both day and night, still the Gospel Temperance meetings were largely attended, and several thousands signed the pledge. I was blessed with the privilege of forming acquaintance with many warm-hearted and earnest workers in the Temperance field, both Christian men and women. I was exceedingly glad to meet here my former pastor and highly-esteemed Christian friend and gentleman, the Rev. Dr. H. B. Ridgeway. I learned that Dr. Ridgeway was highly esteemed not only by his own church and congregation, but by all other citizens who became acquainted with him and his Christian family. Long may he live to blow the Gospel trumpet!

Saturday evening after my arrival in Cincinnati I

was invited by the Vice-President of the Young Men's Christian Association to attend service with him the next day (Sunday) at the county jail, and to speak to the prisoners. The worship began in a social way, and after the opening services I was called upon to address the prisoners, who were seated before me in the chapel. I spoke to them for about twenty minutes, as God gave me the ability, and at the close of the religious exercises one young man seemed to be more deeply impressed and affected than the others; and I was invited by some Christian ladies present to converse with him. I found, to use his own words, he had almost killed his mother by his dissipated life; and now he says, "I am to go to the penitentiary for three years, and all on account of drunkenness; so I desire to obtain the religion you have been speaking about; and I desire your prayers and the prayers of the Christian women and others who meet at the temperance hall this afternoon; so please say to them I am in cell 126." This jail had nearly three hundred cells. We find, as a rule, all throughout the Union that where strong drink is used the most freely, the jails and prisons and lunatic asylums are of the largest size.

I attended the meeting referred to that afternoon at four o'clock, and presented the petition from the young man, and during the meeting many earnest prayers full of faith went up to God in behalf of this young man in cell 126. The next afternoon, Monday, a similar meeting was held. Mrs. Leavitt—one of the original crusade women (God bless her and all her associates!) and one of the number of those who were thrust into jail, in the same city a few years previous, for *obstructing the streets* while praying for liquor sellers—presided at the Gospel Temperance prayer meeting, and during its progress news came from the jail that the young man occupying cell 126 had been converted. Loud hosannas were then sung to God, who hears and answers prayers.

I also visited during my short stay at Cincinnati, the Alms House, as well as some institutions for the punishment of crime, and found the truth verified, which is often uttered by advocates of total abstinence, that about seven-eighths of all the inmates of such institutions in our country, including State prisons and lunatic asylums, are sent there by the effect, directly or indirectly, of the habit of using alcoholic liquors.

I had now been absent from my Eastern home several weeks longer than I anticipated when I left, and the extreme warm weather becoming oppressive, I started for my home, filling several appointments on my way, at Waynesville, Xenia, Ohio; Richmond, Ind.; also at Piqua, Ohio; and at Pittsburgh and Harrisburgh, Pa.; at all of which places the audiences were very large, and fully imbued with the spirit of the great revival of Gospel Temperance spreading all over our land. May He who is leading on His hosts of faithful workers soon lead them to certain victory.

I reached my home at Portland, Maine, on the 20th of July, and found my family well. After a little rest I commenced working for my Master (as I knew he desired my entire life in this Gospel Temperance field), in the towns and cities of New Hampshire, Vermont and Maine, doing what I could to encourage the reformed men to hold fast, and also persuading those who had not signed the temperance pledge to do so, and to become men and Christians. In this work I was greatly blessed in my own soul, and very many testified to the good resulting from my feeble labors.

During my visits to New Hampshire, I became acquainted with many excellent families whose kindness I shall never forget. Among the many I have only to mention the Rev. J. W. Adams and his interesting family, and also Dr. Osborn and his family, of Tilton, all of whom were deeply interested in the Gospel Temperance work.

Of late my heart has saddened to learn that the bright and beautiful little daughter of Brother Adams, aged but three years, has been called to pluck flowers in the garden of Heaven, beyond the tide. The parents and brothers and sister have my sympathy and prayers, that God may supply by His grace and love the place thus made void in their hearts and home.

I desire also to name Rev. C. B. Pitbaldo and family, of Manchester. Brother Pitblado and his wife also are among the most earnest and efficient workers in the Temperance field that can be found in the State. While at Manchester, I had an invitation to give a few of my talks; and was very fortunate in being the guest of Brother Pitblado and his family. Mrs. Pitblado said to me Sabbath morning that she was glad I had come to Manchester, as she desired to visit the inmates of their jails. I was also glad of such a privilege myself and to invite her and other earnest Christian women workers, as well as lay brethren. Presenting ourselves at the door, the Keeper of the jail gave us a welcome admittance. It was soon arranged for us to hold religious service in the women's department of the jail as well as in the men's. On entering the former we found seven young women prisoners, confined there on account of the terrible habit of using intoxicating drinks. Mrs. Pitblado and other Christian women commenced conversation with them in the spirit of sympathy and love, and soon every one of those unfortunates were completely broken in spirit, and commenced crying like a child, and, while earnest prayers, such as are seldom heard, were being offered by the Christian women, the prisoners themselves were heard crying to God for mercy.

This service of intense feeling and power was soon brought to a close, and we were conducted into the men's department of the jail. The men having come out of their cells, were standing against the walls, as no seats had been provided, and we had one of those services of worship made wonderful and glorious by the manifestation of God's power and love; so that while prayer and exhortation were being offered by the Christian women and men, the prisoners were melted to tears, and some of these strong men trembled, and asked to be prayed for. At the close of the service I procured signatures to the Temperance Total Abstinence Pledge of sixteen out of the twenty men prisoners then present.

I also here wish to give an account of one of my visits to Concord, N. H., the capital of the State, and one of the most delightfully situated inland cities of New England. I was invited by Mr. D. H. Ward, a devoted Christian gentleman and earnest and effective laborer in the Temperance cause, who has since been suddenly called to his reward in Heaven, to spend a Saturday and Sabbath to talk to the people about the great question of helping forward the cause of total abstinence. Sabbath afternoon I ascertained that a religious service was held regularly at the State's prison, situated in the city, at four o'clock on each Sabbath, and I expressed a desire to a Christian brother to be present at the prisoners' service. He said he would accompany me, but he doubted if I could gain admittance to the chapel.

On arriving at the Warden's office I was introduced to this State official, the Chaplain of the prison being present, and said to him I desired to attend the services soon to commence, as I was deeply interested in the prisoners of the land. His reply was, that it was not their custom to admit strangers. At this reply of the Warden, the Chaplain intimated that perhaps I might be the Captain Sturdivant that one of the prisoners spoke to him about as living in Maine, and being interested in the outcasts and prisoners. I replied, I presume I might be the one referred to. Upon this the Warden seemed to feel quite different towards me; and said to the Chaplain: "Have the Captain go in and do all the talking, and you defer your sermon to some other time." Of course I would not allow this; but we went into the service, and the Chaplain shortened his excellent sermon so as to give me a few moments to talk to the one hundred and sixty prisoners before me—men for whom Christ died—men from 18 to 80 years of age, who might have done well for themselves and their families and for the world, but for the awful habit and curse of rum drinking.

After the close of the Chaplain's earnest sermon, a hymn was sung by the convicts. As I stepped from the raised platform to the floor and stood in front of the prisoners and in close proximity to them, I noticed near me one young man who seemed terribly broken in spirit while I was talking, and apparently all of them manifested a deep interest in what I was saying. At the close of my talk I asked the prisoners three questions; first:

"How many of you present are in here, directly or indirectly, through the instrumentality of intoxicating liquors, please hold up your hands?"

More than seven-eighths of the prisoners held up their hands.

Second: "Those of you before me who feel sure that you have *mothers* praying for you at home to-day, raise your hands," and with streaming eyes and loud sobs, a large number held up their hands.

Third: "Those of you who desire to be better men, to lead good lives, to become Christians, and desire your speaker and others to pray for you, please hold up your hands."

At this request, also, a large number held up their hands.

That evening I spoke to a large audience in a church. I can never forget this my first visit to Concord, and to the State's prison of New Hampshire.

Nearly two years after this visit to Concord, I was at Old Orchard Beach one day, standing near the depot as the western train arrived. A young man, stepping from the cars, approached me, and gave me his hand, with a hearty grasp of mine, and said :

"Do you remember the afternoon you spoke to the prisoners in Concord State prison ? "

I replied : "Yes ; I do, very distinctly."

" Do you remember of a young man that sat near you as you spoke ? "

" I do."

Said he: " I am the one. I served out my time, and ever since I heard you I have tried to be a Christian; and you will never know, sir—God bless you !—the good you accomplished, under God, that afternoon."

"Cast your bread upon the waters," saith the Scriptures, "and it will return to you after many days." I learned that this was the identical young man who, when he first entered that prison, in conversation with the Chaplain, said he knew of me as one interested in prisoners.

Thus having the unexpected pleasure of seeing this saved young man, at the depot at Old Orchard, brings to mind an incident and a glorious result in the wonderful salvation of one man from the power of moderate drinking, as it is called. At Old Orchard Beach, one Sunday morning, during the progress of the National Christian Temperance Camp-meeting, over which dear Brother Francis Murphy presided, a prayer meeting was in progress, large numbers having early assembled on the beautiful beach, near to God's blue Atlantic. During these services my attention was arrested by some unknown hand pulling my coat. I turned, and saw a lady friend, an earnest Christian Temperance worker, beckoning for my attention. With tears in her eyes, she said : " There is one gentleman in the meeting here who, if you could only persuade him to sign the pledge, will keep it, and become, no doubt, a very effective worker in the cause of total abstinence." At this she pointed the gentleman out to me; and at the close of the morning service I was introduced to him, and found him to be a genial, good-natured and large-hearted man ; so I made it my business to cultivate his acquaintance, and during the forenoon service at the grove we sat near each other. At the close of the noon service, when the invitation was given for people to come forward to the stand and sign the Total Abstinence pledge —I standing at the time near one of the beautiful trees of the grove with pledge book in hand—this gentleman, with others, came to me and asked for the book to sign their names to the Total Abstinence pledge; and while they were affixing their names, shouts and songs went up from the vast multitude, and all joined with heart and lip in singing, "Praise God, from Whom all blessings flow."

At the close of the service, the man who I speak of was one of the most earnest in persuading others to sign the pledge. He was a man well known in the cities of Saco and Biddeford, and hundreds of persons from these cities were present at the camp-meeting that day. When the fact became generally known that O. M. Chadbourne, Esq., had signed the Total Abstinence Temperance Pledge, they could not wait to send the good news to his family, four miles distant by carriage, so they went to the telegraph office, and, on receiving the dispatch, Mrs. Chadbourne and family were soon on their way to the camp-grounds, and that evening had the privilege of hearing the husband and father speak in a Gospel Temperance Prayer Meeting. Brother Chadbonrne has been one of the most earnest and efficient temperance workers in York County since that glad day he signed the pledge, and since the morning the good lady called my attention towards him by gently pulling my coat. "Behold what a *great* matter a little fire kindleth."

In my travels around the country and among the sparsely populated towns, I found some of the greatest heroes of the Nineteenth century among the ministers of the different denominations, with many of whom I became acquainted; and my acquaintance with those self-sacrificing men of God gave me new courage in my work, to which I feel I am callen of God. It is quite a mystery how some of those dear men can live on the little amount they receive, especially where they have a large family. But they have faith that God will provide.

One instance I wish to relate, and also to show the goodness of men who are made poor by drink. I was invited to speak at a small town in New Hampshire. The Methodist minister, Brother Collins, invited me, he being one of the officials of the temperance organization, and, as is usual in such places, the man of all good work. I was his guest. He lived in an unfinished $1\frac{1}{2}$ story habitation, for which he paid thirty-five dollars rent yearly. His wife was an excellent lady; not only did she make her own and her husband's clothes, and the children's also (there being three children), but she used to make quilts and do other hard work for the Sewing Circle, of which she was president; the object was to raise money to help pay the Society's debts. Brother Collins' officials were very liberal with him last year, and voted to raise his salary to *four hundred* dollars—with which the good man would have been perfectly satisfied if he could have *received* even three-quarters of that amount. One of his neighbors, a drinking man, said he liked Brother Collins *very much*, and as he could not get over twenty cents per bushel for his potatoes at the starch mill, he concluded to help Brother Collins out, and so he had sent *his minister* five bushels of potatoes, which he should tell the minister not to credit in his account with the steward, as he made him a present of them.

So I repeat again, these servants of the Most High with their families, many of them are the true heroes of the times in which we live. God bless them! Their mansions in Heaven will be among the most glorious.

During my visit to Washington, and while working with Brother Francis Murphy in that city for a few weeks, trying to get men to abandon the use of strong drink, I was making inquiry one day of a stranger I saw on the street as to how I could best get to the Government printing building. After he gave me the desired information, he said to me: "Captain Sturdivant, I presume you do not know me." I replied I had not the pleasure. He then said: "I was one of the 1,600 men you addressed in the penitentiary last June of a Sabbath forenoon, in Columbus, Ohio; and during your address you urged us to return to our parents, if we had any, as soon as our term of service expired; as no one would be glad to see us and to do for us as our parents, and especially our mothers. I could not get clear of your words, so as soon as my time expired I came home to my mother at once, and I signed the Total Abstinence Pledge, and have since become a Christian man. Am doing well and am happy." As he left me he said: "I owe all this present blessed life to you." I replied: "I am glad for you; but you must give *all* the glory to God."

As I was riding in the street cars one day, in Washington, a colored young man came and spoke to me. I did not recognize him, but replied I was glad to see him. He mentioned the fact that his father had been for a long while with me as cook on one of the steamers I formerly commanded, and also that on one Sabbath I visited a Sunday-school (colored) in Portland, at which time he delivered some appropriate address, with which I was so much pleased that I gave him a gold dollar, and he should never forget me.

At a testimonial meeting given me while in Washington by my Maine friends, this colored friend of mine was present with his associates.

One other significant circumstance is worthy of mention. Brother Murphy had been at work in

Washington two weeks before I arrived there, and had called several times on President Hayes and his excellent wife. One Saturday afternoon I was invited, with a few friends, to call at the White House, as it was Mrs. Hayes' reception day. On entering the room where Mrs. Hayes and others, together with the President, were being introduced to the hundreds of visitors, I found Brother Murphy among the number, and he desired himself the privilege of introducing me, whom he called his benefactor, to Mr. and Mrs. Hayes and others, which he did in a most affectionate and polite manner. I could but remember that about eight years ago I was inclined to speak a kind and encouraging word to Brother Murphy while in a prison cell.

Although after many days God's promises are sure to be fulfilled. Since my return from Washington I have been invited to speak in the Rev. A. Dinmore's Church at Bridgesburg, where I spoke last June. After my address, the pastor rose and said: "I don't suppose the speaker, Brother Sturdivant, ever feels discouraged or has the 'blues,' but if he does, I wish to say, for his encouragement, that there is a man in this audience who was influenced last June by Brother Sturdivant, when he was here to sign the Murphy Total Abstinence pledge ; Brother Sturdivant remarking at the time that he *knew* he would keep the pledge, and he has

kept it, and has also experienced religion, and is
one of the most devoted and active members of
my church." At the close of the service this man
came forward and took me by the hand, which he
warmly grasped, and said he was exceedingly glad
to see me, and longed for the privilege ; said he
owed his present happy life all to me under God ;
also remarked that he was soon to write a history
of his life, in which he should speak kindly of me.

On October 25 we left Portland for our new home
in this City of Brotherly Love, whereunto I was cordially invited by Christian men ; some of whom I
had done business with for many years previous,
they feeling that a man of my disposition, by the
grace of God, and of my experience in the Home
Mission work, and among the prisoners and outcasts,
might accomplish more good for humanity in this
extensive field, which is already white to the har-
vest, than I could in the city where I have lived
and labored for years past, and where the habit of
drinking intoxicants had become quite unpopular.
I am now making this great city the centre of my
labors, feeling that a wise Providence has directed
my steps, and thus I throw myself into this Gospel
Temperance work with an earnest and loving heart,
trusting the Master will make me of some real good
to the poor wanderers in the wilderness of strong
drink, bring them to the Total Abstinence pledge,

and to the foot of the Cross of Christ, where they can find pardon and strength, so that their mothers and wives and children may be more blessed and happy the remainder of their lives.

Almost every day I come in contact with men who have recently been redeemed from the awful curse of rum, and they tell me of their own happiness and the happiness of loved ones at home. Life seems to them new, in fact, when rum-drinking is given up; that old things are passed away, and behold, all things become new. This is the glorious fruit of Gospel Temperance work. Truly, it is the work of the Redeemer of men. I am speaking in the churches mostly, as I think this most important of all Christian work can be best carried forward to complete victory by the churches, the chosen instrumentalities of God for converting the world.

I have spent considerable time in Southern New Jersey, in many small villages and sparsely settled neighborhoods, where Gospel Temperance workers have not often been. In those places I have been greatly blessed, spiritually, in seeing good results. This is what gives us courage to labor on. One poor unfortunate brother was saved from the habit of intoxication, became a total abstainer; yet, feeling his own strength too weak to keep him, he often goes to God, and there finds pardon and strength.

To God be all the glory, of these recent, numerous and wonderful transformations.

I was invited to visit the Town of Cedarville, N. J., and to remain five days and evenings, the people interested having arranged to hold Union Gospel Temperance services for five consecutive evenings in the two churches alternately. The first meeting, Tuesday evening, the audience was large, and at nearly the close, the interest became deeply apparent, so that a goodly number came forward and signed the pledge. The next evening and also the three following evenings were occasions of deep interest and wonderful power, and the results were glorious. Nearly all of the inhabitants of the village came forward and took the pledge of Total Abstinence from all intoxicating drinks.

Our last meeting was to occur Saturday evening. Friday evening, I said to the people: " It seems now as though nearly all of your people have signed the pledge, and I do not see any reason why your only tavern keeper will not be obliged to give up selling intoxicating drink, as he will have no support." Their reply to me was, he will be supported by the poor farmers out the village. Made " poor," I thought, by the curse of rum drinking. I asked if they, the Christian people, had ever visited those poor farmers and their families. They replied, " No; we are sorry to say we have not." I said : "You ought not to let another day pass without going to see them, and get them to sign the pledge, if possible." They asked if I would go with them I replied: "Yes; most cheerfully will I go." We at once chose a committee, and arranged to have the teams to take several persons to visit those poor unfortunates, to be ready the next morning (Saturday). At the hour appointed, a goodly number of Christian women and men started through the cross-roads in the woods to find the hovels and their inmates; and after calling at the dwellings of several drunkards, we came to a poorly-constructed and dilapidated dwelling, and found the inmates at home — the father a poor, degraded drunkard, his wife, and the mother of his children— she a Christian woman—the son a drunkard, the married daughter, with an infant child. And oh, how I pitied her, as, when looking her little innocent in the face, tears fell on its cheek from the eyes of its *discouraged* mother, when she said to me, "The father of my child is a drunkard, and has gone and left me." I could not resist the pleasure of putting into her hand a piece of silver. Several of the neighbors, of the same way of life, had gathered in this residence that forenoon. At first they seemed afraid of us, but soon found we were *their friends*, and had come for their good. The Christian women sang and then prayed; and while those accents were pleading with God, the fountains of the hearts of those inebriates and others were broken up, and after several prayers and songs and personal talks, we presented the pledge and the whole company signed. The dear old mother as she saw her husband and son sign the pledge, her joy seemed to have no bounds. That evening several of the family, including the father and the son, walked into the village to attend our Gospel Temperance service, which closed one of the most beneficial series of meetings I ever attended.

There are many heathens nearer home than China or Japan. May God arouse all His people to hunt them up, and get them to the pledge of total abstinence and to Christ. I shall never forget Brother M. Ewing, who invited me to Cedarville; his kindness and that of his Christian wife, and the dear family who so kindly entertained me and others, will be among my most pleasant memories as I pass along Life's pathway.

The Gospel Temperance work is truly owned and blessed of the Great Originator and Founder of the Gospel; and its results for good are known and seen all over this land. The great reform, originated by Brother Francis Murphy under God nearly two years ago in this great and good city (bad only for the curse of rum), produced most glorious and last-

ing good results, as has also similar kindly labor
which has been done by Gospel Temperance workers
recently. I am glad to see an increased interest
among God's dear ministers and people to help
forward this cause, represented by such men as
John C. Love, W. A. Lowerty, Samuel P. Godwin,
C. Hancock, Capt. Laborn, G. G. Evans, also Mr.
Nesbit, recently redeemed at one of the hundred
meetings held at Eighth Street Church, Philadelphia,
by the Christian Temperance Union, and never
forgetting Mr. John Wanamaker and his fellow
workmen, Wm. Nickols, Johnson and Anderson,
and a host of other laymen, whom I esteem
among my beloved friends ; and while those brethren and others and God's faithful ministers, are
working untiringly in this part of God's moral vineyard, it must not be forgotten that even greater
good in this work is being done by the women of the
Christian Temperance Union of Philadelphia, who
hold public meetings every day and evening in the
week, and not only do they succeed wonderfully in
getting men to the Total Abstinence Pledge, but,
what is far better, hundreds of those poor lost ones,
both men and women, are directed by those
Christian women to seek the pardon and favor of
Almighty God, whose grace they find not only able
to save, but to keep them from the power and dominion of strong drink. Mrs. Whittenmeyer, Mrs.

Tottman and others living in Philadelphia, together with Mrs. Johnson, Mrs. Hart, Mrs. Alford, Miss Pugh, Miss Greenwood and others, of Brooklyn; also Mrs. Partington and Mrs. Johnson, of Providence, R. I.; Mrs. Mulloy and Mrs. Stewart, Miss Frances E. Willard, and also thousands of others with whom I have no personal acquaintance, are all at work in their several spheres of labor; and being better organized and more unselfish and Christ-like, are accomplishing far greater good in helping to rescue the perishing and to lift up the fallen than us poor weak men can do.

While I was in Washington City, during the winter of 1879, by invitation of Brother Francis Murphy to help in the work then progressing under his leadership—he being lead by his great Leader—a mutual friend of ours, Hon. John Lynch, would often say to Brother Murphy: "You ought to go to New York City." I also said the same, feeling an intense desire for the salvation of the tens of thousands of lost brethren in the great city, with its 17 miles of liquor saloons. Brother Murphy at last yielded to his convictions, and went to New York, not by the invitation of any committee, but drawn there by the hope of doing good to the erring and degraded, made so by the curse of strong drink.

He entered upon his work, looking to God for help, and God did most wonderfully bless his labors

in the whole two months or more he was in that vast metropolis. Many thousands were drawn to the pledge, and numbers were converted to God and joined the Church of Christ.

While Brother Murphy was in the midst of his work, it occurred to me I would go and see him, knowing he would be glad (as he always is) to see me. On my arrival at Seventh Street Methodist Church, the place where at the time he was holding his meetings, at the hour of his noon-day Gospel Temperance prayer meeting. I entered quietly, the services having just commenced. After the opening services he discovered me, and sent his loving son Edward to invite me within the altar, and as I entered he extended to me the grasp of his warm hand, at the same time putting one arm around my neck, gave me as tender and loving a kiss as could come from the lips of a mother or wife or sister, saying to the audience, "This is my beloved friend and benefactor, Captain Cyrus Sturdivant." The scene was so touching as to affect many of the audience to tears. I continued to help in this work in New York City for about two weeks as best I could, and while in this work, a call coming from Brooklyn for helpers, it was deemed best for me to go there. We commenced a week in State Street English Lutheran Church, Rev. Mr. Hamer, Pastor, and continued for three weeks and more. The Pastor, Captain H. A. Curtis and other faithful laborers, were greatly encouraged in seeing large numbers taking the pledge and being saved from the habit of using intoxicating drink, and also coming into the Church of the Living God. A similar work was also manifested in York Street M. E. Church, and also in Warren Street M. E. Church and several other churches in different parts of this great City of Churches.

My labors here and in this vicinity constantly increasing, was to me evidence that I ought to make Brooklyn my home and head-quarters, and on May 1st, 1879, we took up our residence at No. 243 Bergen street, near Nevins. I have no doubt this move was the leading of a kind Master, to whose service I have given my time and talents.

I have often expressed the thought and fact that Christian mothers' prayers were being answered, and so helped on the glorious work of transformation among wayward sons. One case among many, to prove this point, I wish to narrate here: While Brother Murphy was laboring in the Seventh Street M. E. Church, Rev. Mr. Gilder, Pastor (God bless him!), there were many interesting conversions. One day a man, apparently 35 years of age, arose in the noon-day prayer meeting, and said: "Three evenings ago, at about nine o'clock, I was in one of the lowest drinking saloons in this city, when, to my surprise, my dear old father entered. I said : 'Father, this is no place for you.' He replied : 'If it is good enough for my only son, it is good enough for me. I have come at the request of your dying mother.'

"'What! my dying mother ?'

"'Yes, my son; as she lay dying, yesterday, her last words to me were, "Go and find William ;" and I have come to find you. I want you to go with me at once to Mr. Murphy's meeting.'

"'At first I hesitated, but the thought of mother's dying words, "Go and find William," was too much for me, and so I came with father, and at the close of the meeting, when the invitation to sign the pledge was given, I came forward tremblingly and put my name to the Total Abstinence Pledge, and as I did so, Mr. Murphy took me by the hand and asked me to kneel down with him and pray. I did so, although to me it was a heavy cross to bear; but I think *then* and *there* God answered my loving mother's prayers, and that I am a new creature in Christ Jesus.' "

Mothers and wives and sisters, pray on ! God hears your cries and counts your tears. There are thousands of such prayers all over this land of ours, from heart-broken ones, ascending to God, and it seems to me they will be answered ere long in some way or other, and the millions of shackled slaves of King Alcohol shall be made free.

A mother whose husband filled a soldier's grave, during the recent Rebellion, came to me one day in Brooklyn, saying she was glad I was giving my life to such a work. She had an only son who was under the dominion of strong drink, and she asked if I would not become interested in him and persuade him to be good, as at the time she thought his conduct would make her crazy. But as yet he shows no signs of reform, and his mother goes about, a living, *dying* monument of despair. This is no isolated case.

I have also became acquainted with a retired ship-master, who said to me, one day, "that he had been in the midst of storms on the sea, but with a good ship under his feet he had no fears. He had a loved brother who used to sail with him, a noble-hearted man. A few months ago this dear brother sickened and died, but with a well grounded hope of a safe harbor in Heaven; and about six weeks ago our son, twenty-six years of age, after a lingering sickness, died and passed on to the better land. His mother and I could feel reconciled to these deaths, but for the last four weeks our only son of twenty years has been brought home every night drunk, and his mother and I have had to sit up for him and put him to bed. This is more than we can bear without God's help; and, oh! do, Brother Sturdivant, pray for us."

Thus it is on every hand, and, knowing these things, we are led to cry, "Oh, Lord, how long! How long, oh, Lord, will Thy people allow this terrible Destroyer to rob us of our brightest and our best?"

During June, 1879, I visited many towns and villages on Long Island, and also on Staten Island, and spoke to the people on this important subject— to me the most important of all subjects—Gospel Temperance. The world will never be brought to Christianity until this soul-destroying, blighting, withering curse shall be annihilated; and this can only be done by the united effort of Christians and good people of this land. May God enable us to realize the great responsibility and power thus committed to our hands, and may we go forth with good courage, trusting in Him who is for us—He is more than all that can be against us.

Our meetings at the eastern end of Long Island, in June, were very interesting, and we trust beneficial, large numbers signing the pledge. At Greenport, Orient, Sag Harbor, Riverhead and other adjacent towns and villages, the people all stirred to activity in this cause of reform. At some of these flourishing towns they hold regular and frequent Gospel Temperance meetings, and the beneficial results are very apparent. I was invited to speak at Orient, a village of about five hundred inhabitants, where they have held a regular temperance meeting every Saturday evening for twenty-six years in one or other of the two churches. The results are—there is no liquor kept for sale, no poor people to be sustained by the town authorities, and the people are so healthy that a physician cannot be sustained. All honor to the beautiful town of Orient, situated by the inland sea at the eastern end of beautiful Long Island. How much more beautiful would Long Island be, if it should be freed from the terrible evil and traffic of intoxicating drink from one end to the other.

Staten Island is so near my home, that it has been very convenient for me to visit it many times, and to speak to the people in the different churches as I have been invited to do by the several ministers. The ministers of the Gospel know full well that the curse of strong drink is the great and powerful hindrance to men's coming to Christ and of accepting the Gospel they preach. In our work to which God has called us, we sometimes meet with discouragements and have the "blues" (only a little, however), as we go forth without any earthly organization to see us and ours fed and clothed, but trusting in God who has called us and His people, that our wants will all be supplied.

A good minister once told me he was astonished at my faith in this matter of support. I replied to him that for years I had been telling people to trust in the Lord, and so had he preached the same Bible doctrine. I was now practicing this trust in God, and He would take care of me and mine. Darkness is only for the night. Light comes with the morning, and so we have light by the way.

On a warm Sabbath in June I was invited by Rev. Brother Hall (who, by the way, had been a sailor) to speak in his church at Woodrow, on Staten Island, in the forenoon, on Gospel Temperance. Owing to the excessive heat, the congregation was not large, but the Lord was with me, and I had real freedom, for I felt at home. At the close of my talk, Brother Hall said I was wholly sustained in my work by voluntary collections on the part of those to whom I spoke, and he then gave the people the privilege of contributing; and at the close of the services, as I was being introduced to and shaking hands with the people, a lady came forward and spoke to her husband, who stood near by me. She said to her husband: "Mrs. B. wishes you to give to Captain Sturdivant for her the sum of twenty dollars. Such a man as he ought to be taken good care of."

This was to me a real surprise, and at first I

could not think it was for me; so, after a little cry
for joy, I wished the donor pointed out to me, but
she had left in her carriage for her elegant home
near by. Those are green spots along the Gospel
Temperance advocate's pathway. The Lord will
provide, and he that casts his bread upon the waters
shall find it after many days.

In my visit to Troy, N. Y., and vicinity, I found
my old and tried friends glad to see me. I spoke
several times in that city and vicinity, and also was
invited to visit Bennington, Vt., and speak twice on
the Sabbath. My visit there to me was very pleasant, and the services in the hall, on Sabbath afternoon, and the union service in the new and beautiful Baptist Church, Rev. Dr. Luther, Pastor (God
bless him!), were seasons of deep interest and spiritual power.

I was invited there by my dear brother in Christ,
W. S. Battersby, and was so kindly entertained by
him and his excellent wife and family, that I shall
never forget my friends in Bennington, Vt.

The Gospel Temperance Union at Troy is one of
the most prosperous within my knowledge. Its power
for good has been wonderful the past two years while
under the presidency of Brother Z. Main, who gave
his time and his money. He was preceded by Brother G. W. Sweet, also a man of powerful influence in the community, and with large heart and full

purse devoted each to the good of the organization.
Brother Miller has recently been elected to fill
Brother Main's place, whose time has expired.
Brother Miller is one of the excellent of earth, and
no doubt success will crown his labors. I have also
visited several towns and villages during July in
Eastern or Northern Connecticut, and find the interest in the temperance work most encouraging.
I spoke to large and interested audiences at New
London, and at Groton ; also at Norwich and Wil-
limantic, Jewett City and Plainfield, and other towns
and villages, at all of which places, the people
treated me very kindly, and I only hope my labors
may prove a real blessing to some one at least. I
have not time or space to mention the names of the
hundreds of real friends, with whom I have become
acquainted in the cities and towns where I have
labored since I gave up all to this Gospel Temperance work. But I am none the less grateful,
their names and deeds of kindness are on my heart.
During the month of August just passed I have visited Pittsburgh, Pa., and labored there and other adjacent cities and towns, and also in some remote
localities ; have renewed my old acquaintance with
many dear friends, and also formed new and valuable acquaintance with many Christian workers, and
also with business men. And during this visit
to the Smoky City, it was pleasing to me to

hear from so many expressions of gratitude to God that Francis Murphy ever came to Pittsburgh. The Old Home Christian Temperance Union at Pittsburgh is a living institution, doing a glorious work in the great city, and sending out its workers, and blessed influence for good in all the country round about. It holds public prayer meetings every day in the week at noon, from 12 to 1 o'clock, and also public Gospel Temperance meetings every evening, and on each Sabbath afternoon. The President, J. R. Hunter, is a true man, completely fitted for the position, as is also his associates in office, and hundreds of co-workers, whose names I shonld be glad to mention, if time and space allowed. Perhaps I ought, in justice, to say that this organization, the Old Home, is fully equal for good results as the Union in Troy, N. Y.

After an extended visit and labor in Pittsburgh and Allegheny, and at several camp-meetings, and also making a trip up the beautiful Monongahela river, on invitation of Captain J. N. Jacobs, he desired me to speak on Gospel Temperance in a chapel at Riverside, seventy-five miles from Pittsburgh. This chapel was built by the Christian mother of Captain Jacobs for union religious services. At the close of the service I held there, Captain Jacobs was the first one to step forward and sign the Total Abstinence Pledge. I returned to Pittsburgh for a few days, and then came to my home in Brooklyn, N. Y., so as to be prepared to fill an appointment on Block Island for September 6 and 7. Coming down the Monongahela river from the trip above named, we made numerous landings with our steamer (I feel quite at home on a good steamboat), some of which landings we made near large distilleries, where whisky is made from the corn and other grain which God designed for food to strengthen man, and not to make that which weakens both body and soul, and sends its victim down to a drunkard's grave. It seemed strange to see hundreds of barrels of whisky thus put on board the steamer, seeking a market, to degrade, impoverish and destroy. I said, Oh, Lord, how long will it be before the people of this country will rise up and put a stop to the manufacture and sale of this awful curse? So, reaching my home in safety, and remaining only a few days with my loved ones, I left for Block Island, which is about 25 miles east-south-east from the westerly end of Rhode Island shore. I took the steamer Ella at Stonington, Conn., and after a few hours of beautiful sail on the ocean, we landed at Block Island. Arrangements were made for Saturday evening and for Sunday forenoon and evening. Block Island is becoming more and more into favor as a public resort in Summer, it being *surrounded* by the broad Atlantic ocean, and the whole

Island nearly (which is three miles in width and nine miles in length) is a continued succession of hills and valleys; and this Island is said to be one of the most healthful on the North Atlantic coast. It has about 1,400 inhabitants, who procure a good living by fishing and also keeping summer boarders. It was the inhabitants of this Island I hoped in God to benefit, and I am happy to say that our meetings were very very interesting and powerful. God seemed to be in our midst, and many hearts were touched, and about sixty persons signed the Total Abstinence pledge. On my leaving, the people would not say good-bye until I promised them I would make them a longer visit in the near future. I lately learned the following temperance fact which occurred in the early history of the settlement of Block Island—nearly two hundred years ago. At that time there came to the Island a man named Arnold. There were on the Island only sixteen English settlers. Arnold brought a barrel of rum and offered it to the Indians, who took it to the top of Beacon Hill, the highest point of land on Block Island. Of the sixteen white settlers only one dared to go up on the hill. His name was Terry, who represented to the Indians and argued with them to prove that Arnold could do nothing for them only to get them drunk; soon the Indians were convinced of this, and manifested a dislike to Mr. Arnold; but it was customary to require some proof that the Indians were sincere. They at once proved their earnestness and sincerity by rolling the barrel of rum down the hill into the valley below, shouting, "Tuckishaw! Tuckishaw! We don't want you—we don't care for you, Mr. Arnold!" By this means the probable massacre was prevented, and the English were at peace. I only wish the good people of this Republic would say to those persons who bring this deadly poison to the cities and towns to sell to our fathers, husbands, brothers and sons: "We don't care for you, and by God's help we will destroy your unrighteous traffic."

On coming to Stonington, Conn., from Block Island, I was invited to speak in the Baptist Church two evenings, and the meetings were largely attended and very interesting. I also spoke to large and interested audiences at Westerly, R. I., and at Mystic Bridge and Noank, Conn., and arrived at my home in Brooklyn safe and well, to remain only a few days, and then go out to fill other appointments, and to help rescue the perishing, and to lift up the fallen ones now in the mire and red stream of intemperance.

And now, dear readers, in closing this short narrative, written in haste, and referring the readers to some letters and testimonials and facts, as evidences of what some other persons besides my poor self think of me and my past work, I sincerely ask for your prayers and sympathy that my life may be useful, and that when the Angel of Death comes to me, it will find me with the harness on, fighting the greatest enemy to human happiness, unless before Death approaches he may have been conquered.

Your affectionate Brother and Friend,

CYRUS STURDIVANT.

BROOKLYN, December, 1879.

APPENDIX.

[Extract from the Minutes of the Philadelphia Methodist Episcopal Preachers' Meeting, held September 16th, 1878.]

Resolved, That there is as great a necessity as ever for earnest and faithful workers in the cause of Gospel Temperance, and that we are as much as ever devoted in spirit and practice to this great work.

We, therefore, take very great pleasure in commending to all our Ministers and Churches Capt. CYRUS STURDIVANT, a man, by sympathy, zeal and piety, admirably adapted to this glorious work; and that we pledge ourselves to assist him in entering every open door and pray for his greatest possible success in helping men to a life of sobriety, virtue, usefulness and happiness.

NATHAN B. DURELL,
Secretary.

The National Christian Temperance Union, which for several weeks past has been holding a series of very successful temperance meetings at the church on Eighth street, below Buttonwood, held a meeting last evening at Grace Methodist Episcopal Church, Broad and Master streets. An immense audience, the largest ever gathered in the church, was present. On the platform were Select Councilman Miskey and Mr. Jas. Long, President of the Board of Education. Captain Cyrus Sturdivant related in a speech full of pathos the story of Francis Murphy's redemption. During the recital a large number of the audience were affected to tears. William A. Laverty and John C. Love made speeches, and related many touching anecdotes of the reformation of fallen men. Mr. Jas. Clark sang temperance songs, and Mr. Long made an appeal for a generous contribution to help on the cause, which was liberally responded to.—*Philadelphia Times, Jan. 7, 1878.*

A Presbyterian minister, whose heart yearns for a revival in his church, says : "The people in my place cannot afford a revival. There is $100,000 worth of liquor sold over the counter in our village annually. The very men whom we desire to reach with a revival are in one way or another concerned in the business and profits of the traffic. They cannot afford to have a revival—it would cost them too much."

Mrs. E. L. Comstock says that she has visited 115,000 prisoners in the prisons of the United States the last eighteen years, and out of that number 105,000 were brought there directly or indirectly through liquor.

Gospel Temperance meetings, under the leadership of Capt. Sturdivant, of Philadelphia, have been in progress during the past week at the State Street Lutheran Church, and last evening the most interesting one of the series was held. Captain Sturdivant presided, and opened the meeting by calling upon several present to lead in prayer. Singing followed, and was succeeded by speeches from Mr. Hill, Mr. Knight, Mr. Whitney and Dr. Hanna, pastor of the church. The speeches were characterized by great earnestness of spirit, and were listened to with great attention. The performance of Mr. Walsh on the banjo was enjoyed by the audience, as was the speaking of Mr. Jones, a missionary from New York. The enthusiasm reached its highest when signers to the pledge affixed their names and received the Murphy badge. There were a number of young men and several little girls who affixed their names to the promise. The services closed at 10 o'clock, when it was announced that Colonel Caldwell would speak to-morrow afternoon, Mrs. Van Cott on Monday afternoon, and Miss Anna Oliver on Monday evening. Wednesday afternoon Francis Murphy will be present, and Mr. and Mrs. Wilson will sing. Other speakers will be present during the week, and the meetings will be made as agreeable as possible. Dr. Hanna, the pastor, extended a cordial invitation to the reformed men who had signed the pledge to attend the services to-morrow, and the meeting was closed with singing. Captain

Sturdivant is the gentleman who was the means of reforming Mr. Murphy, and has been for years engaged in Gospel Temperance work. He is a warm-hearted, kindly man—is zealous in his efforts, which should enlist the temperance people in the city. The meetings will be held at this church afternoons and evenings during the coming week, and all are invited to attend.—*Brooklyn Eagle.*

TO THE PRESS.

Captain Cyrus Sturdivant, of Philadelphia, Pa., who was the instrument through whom Francis Murphy was saved, is about to open a Gospel Temperance Meeting in our city. He is worthy of the fullest confidence, and I doubt not will accomplish a good work here. Permit me to recommend him to your good offices:

W. C. STEELE,
Pastor 53d Street M. E. Church.

BROOKLYN, Nov. 28, 1873.

Captain Cyrus Sturdivant, of Portland, will address the Reform Club on "Evils of Intemperance" and "Benefits of Home Mission Work," next Friday evening. Captain S. has spoken in Lancaster before, and is one of the most interesting temperance lecturers we have ever heard. He is now devoting his whole time to the cause, asking only such compensation as may be voluntarily contributed.—*Lancaster (Pa.) Gazette, Aug. 8, 1878.*

Captain Sturdivant, the gentleman who was instrumental in the conversion of Francis Murphy, the great temperance reformer, gave very interesting lectures on the subject of temperance, on Sunday afternoon, in Wilson's Hall, and in the evening at the First M. E. Church. The congregations on both occasions were exceedingly large, and the remarks of Captain Sturdivant were very affecting, highly interesting, and were very well received by his large and attentive audiences.—*Vineland (N. J.) Journal, January 13, 1878.*

COMPLIMENTARY TO MY BROTHER.

BY REV. GEORGE TAYLOR, OF ILLINOIS.

C o-worker with the great deliverer ;
Y our mission, as a messenger of grace,
R eaching out the helping hand of kindness
U nto the helpless fallen of our race :
S earching out the poor forlorn inebriate,
S oothing the heart-pangs of his wretched home,
T urning from the paths of sin the straying
U nto Jesus, who bids the wanderer come.
R ejoice, my brother, in thy God-appointed work;
D ivinely honored he whom thus our blessed Lord
I nvites to duty; *He* will your labors bless.
V erily, above all price shall be thy reward.
A t the feet of Jesus, then, lay down each trophy,
N e'er forgetting one, your brightest—Francis Murphy.
T o God alone be given all the glory.

A Temperance meeting will be held in the First Baptist Church of this city, on Sunday evening, March 24, commencing at 7 o'clock. The meeting will be addressed by Captain Cyrus Sturdivant, formerly of Portland, Maine.

During the past year Captain Sturdivant has been laboring in the States of Pennsylvania, Ohio and Indiana, also New Hampshire, Vermont and Maine, helping in the great Murphy Gospel Temperance movement that is producing under God such wonderful conversions of many thousands of the intemperate. Captain S. will give a condensed history of this great work, and also incidents and interesting facts connected therewith, if desired by the people whom he is invited to address. Captain S. was the humble instrument, under God, of helping Francis Murphy to a new life, in the city of Portland, State of Maine, in the year 1870; and will give an account of the wonderful conversion of this apostle of Temperance on Sunday evening next.

Capt. Sturdivant makes no stipulated charge for his services, unless desired, but expects voluntary contributions to sustain him in his work, to which he devotes his whole time, helping to "rescue the perishing and lift up the fallen."—*Bridgeton (N. J.) Chronicle, March* 27, 1878.

Wednesday last brought Captain Cyrus Sturdivant and a fellow-laborer, Captain Leabourn, unexpectedly to Ocean Grove. They had been working in the cause of temperance at Freehold, and took advantage of an off-evening to visit our city by the sea, a place neither of them had ever seen before.

The Tabernacle was placed at their service, hand-bills struck off announcing a meeting, and at 7½ o'clock these zealous fellow-laborers were greeted with a good congregation, which soon increased to large proportions, considering the lateness of the season.

Capt. Leabourn was the first to address the audience. He told the sad tale of wasted years, over twenty of which he had been an infatuated drunkard. From the beginning of temptation when a youth, downward ever, his course ran until, forsaken by wife, children and friends, he staggered into a Murphy meeting one night in Philadelphia, and encouraged by the brotherly sympathy of that apostle of reform, his almost paralyzed hand, that had often wielded the sword in patriotic devotion to the Union, signed the Murphy pledge. He also bowed his knees and implored help from God, to keep it, and had remained steadfast, with a new life opening around him, and again in the bosom of his little family.

He is a fine, earnest speaker, and made a deep impression.

Captain Sturdivant followed with a circumstantial account of the conversion of Francis Murphy, while a prisoner in the jail at Portland, Maine. This story, referred to so often by Murphy himself, who attributes his salvation, under God, to the labors of Sturdivant, was given by the latter with thrilling minuteness, and his rousing appeal to those present to work for the uplifting of the fallen everywhere, met with a ready response.

After the people were allowed the privilege to give a collection to help the brethren on in their efforts, Jennie Smith, with whom they were guests, gave an interesting statement of temperance and Gospel work in the West, and begged all young ladies to exert their influence in favor of saving men from the ruinous habits of intoxicating drink. The result was that over fifty persons signed the pledge.—*Ocean Grove Record.*

An earnest, devoted and self-sacrificing man, a practical Christian, one of those whose lives shine in good deeds to their fellow-men, is Captain Cyrus Sturdivant, who delivered a lecture before the Temperance Union last evening. The hall was crowded, and the closest attention was given to Captain Sturdivant, in a speech of upwards of an hour, save when he was interrupted by outbursts of applause. The speaker stated what seemed to be a pleasant experience of general extent in the present temperance movement. The various Christian churches engaged in this work break down the partition walls which have hitherto kept them apart, and a kinder feeling for each other, a larger fellowship, is produced. Mr. Sturdivant gave a history of the conversion of Mr. Francis Murphy in Portland, Maine, several years ago. The narrative was very affecting, and interesting in the extreme. Mr. Sturdivant urged upon the Union the great importance of establishing a Holly Tree Inn. A vote of thanks was tendered the lecturer and a collection taken for him.

. After the conclusion of his lecture, he introduced Mr. Geo. G. Evans, of Philadelphia, who made a few interesting remarks. Mr. Evans will be remembered as the gift book man. He amassed a fortune in his business.—*Titusville Herald*, *June* 20, 1878.

Saturday forenoon's session of the Temperance Camp-meeting at Sterling consisted of a prayer meeting, led by Captain Cyrus Sturdivant, of Portland, Me. At 1 o'clock in the afternoon another prayer meeting was held in Grace Church tent. At 2 P. M. began the Reform Club meeting at the main stand, which was beautifully decorated for the occasion with evergreens, flowers and mottoes, surrounding a picture of Francis Murphy. The exercises were opened with reading of Scriptures and prayer by Rev. Mr. Dustin, of Berlin, after which Mr. Booth welcomed the Reform Clubs, and introduced Major F. G. Stiles, President of the Worcester Reform Club, as presiding officer of the afternoon. After an introductory address by President Stiles, speeches followed by George P. French, of Clinton; Major Ross and Joel Smith, of Leominster; Mr. Wellington, of Spencer; A. P. Rice and Messrs. Smith and

Crooks, of Worcester; Pliny B. Southwick and Rev. Mr. Dustin, of Berlin, and Messrs. Smith, of South Gardner, Paul, of Oxford, Johnson, of West Boylston, and Eames, of Lancaster, all members of Reform Clubs.

Sunday the attendance was very large, especially in the afternoon, when there were between five and six thousand persons present. Speeches were made in the forenoon by Col. Luther Caldwell, of Elmira, N. Y.; Captain Cyrus Sturdivant, of Portland, Me., and Mr. R. T. Booth. In the afternoon the meeting was one of the largest ever held upon the grounds, the noon extra train from Worcester bringing out a numerous delegation, as well as the trains from Nashua and Fitchburg. The exercises were opened with the reading of the parable of "The Good Samaritan," by Mr. Booth, after which prayer was offered by Captain Sturdivant. D. S. Simons, of Greenfield, the converted landlord, was then introduced, and related some of his experiences. He said he had been a rum-seller 30 years, but February 14 last he signed the pledge, and had since stood by it.

Col. Caldwell was next introduced, and delivered his lecture in defence of Christianity as a reforming power in the world, in reply to Col. Ingersoll. He said the two greatest evils now in the world were intemperance and infidelity, which went hand in hand. The Christian religion was the greatest foe of both, and would in the end conquer both.

The speeches were interspersed with singing by the chorus choir, led by Mr. Prescott, of Nashua. A meeting was also held in the evening, with addresses by several reformed men. The meetings will be continued to-day and to-morrow forenoon. —*Worcester Spy, September* 9, 1878.

Our former citizen, Captain Cyrus Sturdivant, was in the city yesterday on a flying visit. He is looking nicely and feels excellently. He is devoting his whole time to Gospel Temperance work, in which he is meeting with glorious success. He arrived in the city Wednesday evening, and left for Philadelphia last evening, from whence he will go to New York and assist Francis Murphy in his meetings there, next week.—*Portland Press.*

TO WHOM IT MAY CONCERN.

I take great pleasure in recommending to the churches and the friends of humanity, Captain Cyrus Sturdivant, of Brooklyn, N. Y., as a competent, earnest and worthy advocate of Gospel Temperance, whose long experience and abilities enable him to present this great cause to the people in a convincing and successful manner.

W. H. BOOLE.

SOUTH NORWALK, Feb. 10, 1879.

[From the Washington National Union, February, 1878.]

TESTIMONIAL RECEPTION TO THE SAILOR EVANGELIST— SPEECHES BY CAPTAIN STURDIVANT, REPRESENTATIVE LINDSEY, EX-GOVERNOR AUSTIN, FRANCIS MURPHY, CAPTAIN JOHNS AND OTHERS—CONGRESSIONAL ENDORSEMENT OF CAPTAIN CYRUS STURDIVANT.

The sons and daughters of the Pine Tree State gathered to a goodly number to do honor to one of her noblest citizens, at the Metropolitan Church, last night. The reception testimonial tendered to Captain Cyrus Sturdivant was the occasion of an exceedingly good time being had by all present. The hearty appreciation of his old friends and neighbors must have gladdened the heart of the philanthropic old sea-captain beyond power of expression.

The proceedings were opened by prayer, followed by a hymn from Mr. and Mrs. Wilson. Hon. W. B. Snell presided, and in the name of the citizens of Maine stated their intention was to honor Captain Sturdivant, for his influence on religion and temperance revivals. He had received testimonials from many of the best of the citizens of Maine; from Governor Connor, the present executive officer of the State. No man could be Governor of that State if not known to be a devoted temperance man. He read the following letter from Hon. W. P. Frye, which explains itself:

Messrs. W. B. Snell and A. P. Knight and others of the Committee:

"I am very sorry to decline your invitation to participate in the meeting this evening for the benefit of Captain Sturdivant, but an imperative engagement compels me to do so. Permit me, however, to assure you that I sympathize heartily with the purposes announced. I know Mr. Sturdivant well, by reputation. His fidelity, earnest devotion and Christian charity are recognized through the length and breadth of my State. His kind hand lifted many poor drunkards from their degradation, his good words giving them strength to overcome and to endure. He has brought light into the darkness of many homes, joy into the sadness of many hearts. You do well to bid him 'God speed.' I have enclosed evidence of practical sympathy which will more than compensate for my absence.

"Very respectfully,

WM. P. FRYE."

Hon. S. D. Lindsey, of Maine, spoke of the influence of prohibition in his State. He said that no man could hope to obtain a standing in society who was not a strict temperance man. This was only obtained after long and arduous labor. The people there were so strict that even the respectable drug store would not sell liquor on a prescription.

"Jesus, Lover of My Soul," was then rendered by Mr. and Mrs. Wilson with excellent effect.

Captain Cyrus Sturdivant was next introduced, and said he was very grateful for this privilege of becoming better acquainted with the people of Washington, and especially of those residents here who hailed from his own native State. He little thought a score of years ago, when the founders of this beautiful church were in Maine soliciting donations in aid of its completion, and he had given his mite towards that end, that he should ever stand there in the character that he did to-night. In this connection he alluded to the departure of Dr. Newman, its pastor, from the Metropolitan Church, and said that his only regret was that he could not make Dr. Newman a metropolitan preacher and keep him here. The speaker then reviewed his life for the past twelve years, when he had first commenced his work in the Lord's vineyard a missionary at Portland, and it was then that he first felt a deep interest in the women and children who were suffering from their husbands' and fathers' terrible habits of intemperance, and since the great revival in that reform he had brought glad tidings and good news to many poor wanderers from the paths of temperance. From that time it seemed his only alternative to devote his whole life to this noble work.

He spoke at some length of the conversion of Francis Murphy seven years ago through his efforts, with the help of God, and related with ill-concealed emotion the affecting scenes surrounding the death of the wife of that now famous temperance advocate.

Mr. Sturdivant reverted to other instances of the powers of kindness and prayers on the most hardened sinners, and said he was not weary of the work of saving souls from the demon of alcohol, and hoped God would make him the instrument of saving more men from the evil results of strong drink. He promised to be diligent in this field, and would be glad to know that the citizens of Washington wished him to remain here, in which case he would labor till the enemy was dead and the Lord spared him.

Ex-Governor Austin made an eloquent speech, in which he paid a hearty tribute to the worth and work of Capt. Sturdivant. He said that Maine was not so much known for her forests and snows, or any natural feature, as for her prohibition. The men of to-day have seen the same dissipation in that State, in their boyhood, that now exists in this and other places where license is the rule. He did not, however, believe that to obtain a prohibition law in every State, irrespective of the opinions of the people, would be a good thing. He remembered the fierce fight necessary to establish it in Maine. It was seldom that a conviction could be obtained against offenders at first, as the public sentiment was then against prohibition; but after the first conviction they had no more difficulty in enforcing the law. He would insure a hearty reception for Captain S. and Mr. Murphy in the West, and no opposition would occur, he was sure. Liquor selling would yet be made a crime all over the land. But, preliminiary work being necessary, it must be done by such men as are now doing it in this city.

Mrs. Wilson then sang a solo, "The Golden Gates of Heaven," her clear and flexible voice ringing welcome echoes in the hearts of the delighted audience. Mrs. Wilson would make a mark in any department of vocalism, though her style seems peculiarly adapted to the class of work her conviction suggests.

Captain H. J. Johns, of Minnesota, then spoke. He did not understand why he was there, except, being a captain, to bear Captain S. company. He characterized the President's reception of the procession on Friday last as very significant. He recognized in it the elements of a greater reform than even his glorious efforts in the South would ever bring. He referred in touching terms to Captain Sturdivant's humane efforts, and especially his aid to Murphy and such as he was when the Captain found him. The Washington or Galt revival was thorough, and, at the time the excitement was at its height, it was considered disreputable to have wine on the sideboard. The reaction that ensued would never have happened if the Church had taken hold of the subject in time.

Mr. Murphy, his son, Rev. Dr. Rankin and Col. Gray entered at this stage, amid vociferous applause.

"Hail! The Great Emancipator!" was sung by Mr. and Mrs. Wilson.

Col. Gray spoke for a short time. He said that Maine had set a good example to other States and nations, and Maine men to all the world.

Mr. Murphy said he was glad to accept the invitation to be on the platform at this testimonial to his beloved friend and brother, and to be able to speak some words of cheer and comfort to him. He spoke of the sacrifices made by the men of Maine in peace and war. He was proud of being an adopted citizen of Maine; he was proud of her sons and daughters, who have never been bought or sold. He said that, though a Democrat, when he heard that Mr. Blaine had not been nominated he wept like a child. He spoke in eulogistic terms of Hons. W. P. Frye, T. B. Reed and other Maine men well known in Congress.

There were at home men just as celebrated for their virtues as any who came here. Among all those great men, there was not a greater benefactor than his friend, Captain Sturdivant. Starting on his beneficent career with ample wealth, he now stood homeless. At home he never met him on the street when he had not something in his hand carrying to some poor, miserable creature. The kind words spoken there by those good Christian gentlemen were more welcome than any other testimonial that could be presented to him. He closed with a glowing tribute to, and painted a hopeful picture of the future work of the philanthropic man whom they had met to honor.

The singing of the doxology and the giving of the benediction closed the meeting at about 10 o'clock P. M.

The following letter from ex-Governor Parham, of Maine, will be read with interest:

PORTLAND, October 25, 1877.

To whom this may concern:

I have known the bearer, Capt. Sturdivant, for many years as an earnest worker in the cause of Temperance. He has devoted himself especially to the interest of the poor and unfortunate, and the reformation of criminals. His work in the Allen Mission, and the Jail in Portland, has been peculiarly praiseworthy and remarkably successful, and has secured the good-will of all who are familiar with his efforts.

SIDNEY PARHAM.

The following letter is from Joshua Nye, Insurance Commissioner of Maine; also member of Centennial Commission:

AUGUSTA, October 23, 1877.

To whom it may concern:

This may certify that the bearer, Captain Cyrus Sturdivant, has always been one of the prominent and successful Christian and Temperance workers in Maine. His prison work has brought many souls to Christ, who had become hardened in sin. His Christian efforts in the Portland Jail gave to the world that grand temperance reformer, Francis Murphy. His labors in Portland, in the Allen Mission, has been the means of binding up many a wounded heart, and bring them to put their trust in Christ. I love him as a brother, and ask the sympathy of all people wherever he may be called to labor.

JOSHUA NYE.

PHILADELPHIA, PA., July 24, 1877.

It is an unspeakable pleasure for me to introduce to your most favorable consideration my dearest and best friend, Captain Cyrus Sturdivant, who brought me to our merciful Redeemer; and He held me, blessed be His name. My benefactor consecrated himself and all that he had years ago to the cause of God, and to His poor children; he had a competency, but, in the midst of suffering, hunting up God's poor in prison, and elsewhere finding them in great need, he could not but give them help. This he has practiced, to my own knowledge, for many years, until he gave "all that he had." He is to-day without a place, however, to lay his head, depending upon the generosity of God's people where he is called to labor. I beseech you, deal bountifully with him. He is eminently worthy of all we can do for him. He has been a blessing to mankind. Hear him, he lives in the fullness of the Gospel of Christ. Any kindness extended him will be considered a personal favor to your brother in Christ,

FRANCIS MURPHY.

———

CINCINNATI, July 10, 1877.

To the Friends of Temperance everywhere, we send greeting :

Capt. Cyrus Sturdivant, of Portland, Maine, who, upon invitation from our ex-committee, has been lecturing for us to our edification and instruction, now leaves us for other fields of labor. We take the opportunity of testifying to his Christian and gentlemanly deportment among us, and commend him to all Christian and temperance people everywhere as an earnest and faithful servant of the Master, and loving friend of the depraved and fallen creatures of humanity, the salvation of whose souls he is so earnestly laboring for. May God's richest blessing accompany his humble efforts.

Very respectfully, yours in Christ,

J. WILLARD GRUBBS, *Secretary.*

———

PHILADELPHIA, May 30, 1877.

To Ministers and Members of the Christian Church :

I have known Capt. Cyrus Sturdivant for about ten years, and have had large business transactions with him, amounting to over $100,000, all of which were perfectly satisfactory.

While very active and diligent in business, he carried on a very useful mission in Portland, Me., visiting the sick, and supplying the wants of the poor, preaching both in prison and in his own Mission Chapel. In these labors he was instrumental in the conversion of Francis Murphy, and is now working with him in the greatest temperance movement of the country. He is worthy of all confidence, and will be made a blessing to the people wherever he goes, and I trust he will meet with a generous reception in all the churches.

REV. JAMES NEILL.

————

COATICOOK, P. Q., September 5, 1877.

It was our pleasure to hear Brother Sturdivant last evening. In our opinion the good Lord has called and qualified him to go forth into the vineyard as a Temperance Evangelist.

We wish him much success in his good work, and bespeak for him the kind offices of all the lovers of moral reform.

ALEX. HARDIE,
Pastor of Methodist Church.

————

STANSTEAD, P. Q., CANADA, October 22, 1877.

To whom it may concern :

I desire most cheerfully to bear testimony to the value and usefulness of the services of Captain Cyrus Sturdivant while visiting us in Stanstead and in Derby Line, Vt. His addresses, five in number, were clear, earnest expositions of true Gospel Temperance, enforced by many beautiful and powerful illustrations. Many were induced to take the pledge of total abstinence. The Captain's visit has been beneficial and encouraging to old workers, and the means of good to many others. The Ladies of the Women's Temperance Union concur with me in this commendatory note, and we pray to God to bless Brother Sturdivant in his work of faith and love.

WM. SCOTT,

Minister in charge of the Methodist Church; and ex-President of the Montreal Conference.